Preface

When I think of how my study of how to be generationally savvy began, it was conversation by conversation. The first was a problem-solving conversation with my superintendent, who was curious about ways to support the district as increasing numbers of administrators retired and replacements came in quickly. That first conversation led me to design an in-district administrator retreat. The feelings about the topic, both skeptical and curious, were anything but indifferent, and opinions were voiced. This topic had heat. Something was up.

As I crafted the "Being Generationally Savvy" workshop time and time again during the next few months, outside the district and then across the country, I added to my stockpile of stories people told me at coffee breaks and noted the questions people asked as they tried to apply the work in their contexts. I held focus groups after school for different generations to tell me their challenges collaborating with others at work. I brought in lunches for new teachers so they could tell me about their struggles and share what supports they needed. And then the e-mails would come. "Have you seen this article?" or "You have to hear this story from an interview I just did yesterday with this new teacher—such a generational moment!"

The set of questions grew. People pushed and pulled at the generational filter I was describing. How did being generationally savvy change for those in an urban setting? Did it matter as much in a rural setting? What about the filter of culture? Of gender? What about the developmental stages? Wasn't everyone going to change and become like a Traditionalist at age 65?

The work went deeper. Specific requests for assistance helped develop the topic even more.

- What about Millennial supervisors and administrators? What do we do for them since they are so much younger than those they will be leading and evaluating?
- What can we do to create a better succession plan, because we can see our district will have more retirements in the next 10 years?
- What can we do to recruit new employees so they think this is a great place to work? Do we need to change our orientation? What other changes do we need to make?

- What can we do to support veteran teachers as we increase expectations around technology and other new initiatives that change how people will work together? How will we support them in changes that are likely to be uncomfortable?
- How do we talk to 40-somethings who feel so different than Boomers? Do we need to change our policies for them and the Millennials?
- What about professional development? Should we do more online? What needs to be taught face-to-face?

And so this book was written. It compiles the discussions and the research, the e-mails and the articles, the focus groups and the coffee breaks. This book *is* the conversation. Join in.

—*Jennifer Abrams*

Acknowledgments

Much appreciation goes to the following people who sensed the need for discussion around this topic and who have supported me in ways they might never truly know. I am grateful.

To Mary Frances Callan, my former superintendent, Burton Cohen, my former director of secondary education, Becki Cohn-Vargas, my former director of elementary education, and others at Palo Alto Unified School District who offered me a space to talk about generational challenges and a forum in which to work with the material.

To those in other school boards and school districts and educational organizations who added to and pushed the work forward: Judy Levinsohn and her new-teacher mentors at Orange County Office of Education; Caroline Satoda and Debra Eslava-Burton and their colleagues at San Francisco Unified School District; Anna Moore and others at Monterey County Office of Education; Sharon Ofek and her new teachers at Jane Lathrop Stanford Middle School; Michael Zeldin, Chaim Heller, and others in the DeLeT Program community; the Association of California School Administrators; the Independent Schools Association of the Central States; the California Association of Independent Schools; the Virginia Association of Independent Schools; the Illinois Principals Association; and those at Learning Forward conferences who encouraged me, participated in the workshops, and shaped my thinking.

To my colleagues outside the United States with whom I have worked and who found the ideas "right on" and worthy of consideration: Scott Moreash, Luciana Cardarelli, Suzanne Molitor, Hilda Pierorazio, and others in Peel District School Board (DSB) in Mississauga, Ontario, Canada; Clara Howitt and others at Greater Essex County DSB in Windsor, Ontario, Canada; members of Tri-Association: The Association of American Schools of Central America, Colombia, Caribbean and Mexico; and members of the East Asia Regional Council of Schools. This work has deepened and broadened thanks to your perspectives.

To my "behind the scenes" supporters, friends, and family who were my cheerleaders and brought me generational perspectives of all ages: my father, Richard Abrams; my late mother, Myrna Abrams; my Gen-Xer brother and sister-in-law, Adam and Shelley Abrams; and my "not yet to be generationally named" nephews,

Joe and Evan. To my friends of all generations, John Hebert, John Fredrich, Jen Wakefield, Greg Matza, Ann Idzik, Sean O'Maonaigh, Pam Lund, Collene Bliss, Katy Bimpson, and Mary Sano, who generously listened, dinner after dinner, walk after walk, as I crafted the workshop, and ultimately the book, and who offered much needed perspective. To the Kimpton Hotels where Valerie and I wrote parts of this book and spent many a fabulous evening, and to our kind and supportive editor, Dan Alpert. It was Dan who introduced me to my coauthor, Valerie, my Joneser colleague, who through her agile and sharp writing skills made this book so much more engaging and thoughtful.

—Jennifer Abrams

I feel a deep gratitude to the many, many great teachers who taught me not only their subjects but also to love learning. Many of them may not be with us anymore, but their names stay with me as inspirations and people whose guiding hands at key times in my life shaped me: Sr. Mary Agnes, Mrs. Dohn, and Mrs. Sunseri at Ursuline Academy in Bethesda, Maryland; Mrs. Crayhan at Barnsley Elementary in Rockville, Maryland; Mrs. Mills and Mrs. Goodman at Wood Junior High in Rockville, Maryland; Maryanne Williams and Dianne Emanuel at Wilson High School in Florence, South Carolina; and so many others.

The National Staff Development Council (NSDC) contributed so much to my professional learning during nearly a decade as editor of the *JSD* and through numerous conferences that helped deepen my understanding of the field, and I am thankful for the opportunities I had to learn with NSDC, now Learning Forward. Thank you to Dennis Sparks and Joan Richardson, who were going to hire someone from Ohio and instead allowed me to join the NSDC family in 2000, and to Stephanie Hirsh and Joellen Killion, who have continued my learning.

I feel a deep appreciation to my family, particularly Hannah and Grace, who watched unflinchingly as I inched my way through this work.

Finally, I am everlastingly grateful to Dan Alpert, whose unfailing understanding and faith in this book allowed it to happen, and to Jennifer for inviting me in so willingly to be a part of it.

—Valerie A. von Frank

About the Authors

Jennifer Abrams is a national and international education and communications consultant for schools and hospitals. Jennifer trains and coaches teachers, administrators, support specialists, nurses, hospital personnel, and others on successful instructional practices, new-employee support, supervision and evaluation, being generationally savvy, having hard conversations, and effective collaboration skills.

In Palo Alto Unified School District (Palo Alto, California), Jennifer was a professional developer who designed training for new teachers, K–12 teachers, instructional supervisors, and administrators in areas of instruction, equity, supervision, and teacher leadership. She also was lead coach for the Palo Alto-Mountain View-Los Altos-Saratoga-Los Gatos Consortium's Beginning Teacher Support and Assessment Program.

Her publications include *Having Hard Conversations* published by Corwin in 2009, "Planning Productive Talk," an article for ASCD's *Educational Leadership* (October 2011), the chapter, "Habits of Mind for the School Savvy Leader" in Art Costa's and Bena Kallick's book, *Learning and Leading With Habits of Mind: 16 Essential Characteristics for Success*, and contributions to the book *Mentors in the Making: Developing New Leaders for New Teachers* published by Teachers College Press.

Jennifer has been featured in ASCD's video series *Master Class*, hosted by National Public Radio's Claudio Sanchez, as a generationally savvy expert for "Tune in to What the New Generation of Teachers Can Do," published in *Phi Delta Kappan*, May 2011, and by the Ontario Ministry of Education for its *Leadership Matters: Supporting Open-to-Learning Conversations* video series.

Jennifer considers herself a "voice coach," helping others learn how to best use their voices—be it collaborating on a team, presenting in front of an audience, coaching a colleague, or supervising an employee. She lives in Palo Alto, California. Jennifer can be reached at jennifer@jenniferabrams.com or www.jenniferabrams.com.

Valerie von Frank is an author, editor, and communications consultant. A former newspaper editor and education reporter, she has focused much of her writing on education issues, including professional learning. She served as communications director in an urban school district and a nonprofit school reform organization and was the editor of *JSD*, the flagship magazine for the National Staff Development Council, now Learning Forward, for seven years. She has written extensively for publications, including *JSD*, *Tools for Schools*, *The Learning System*, *The Learning Principal*, and *T3*. She is coauthor with Ann Delehant of *Making Meetings Work: How to Get Started, Get Going, and Get It Done* (Corwin, 2007), with Linda Munger of *Change, Lead, Succeed* (NSDC, 2010), and with Robert Garmston of *Unlocking Group Potential to Improve Schools* (Corwin, 2012).

Introduction: Lost in Translation

You might be experiencing a "generational moment" if:

- You pat yourself on the back for getting on Facebook, only to find everyone is now tweeting and tumbling.
- You give someone your e-mail address and get a strange look when you get to the @aol.com ending.
- You hear from a teacher that you need to get the staff meeting over early because she has to pick up her kids.
- You invite an intern to a meeting only to have him offer you suggestions about how it could be run better.
- You get an inbox full of "reply all" e-mails to your department chair's request for an RSVP.
- You have no idea what RSVP stands for—or why you should care.

If you haven't noticed that you're working with multiple generations, then you haven't looked up from your desk lately. For the first time ever—many people say—there are *four* generations at work in many organizations.

Consider these workforce demographics for the United States and Canada from 2010:

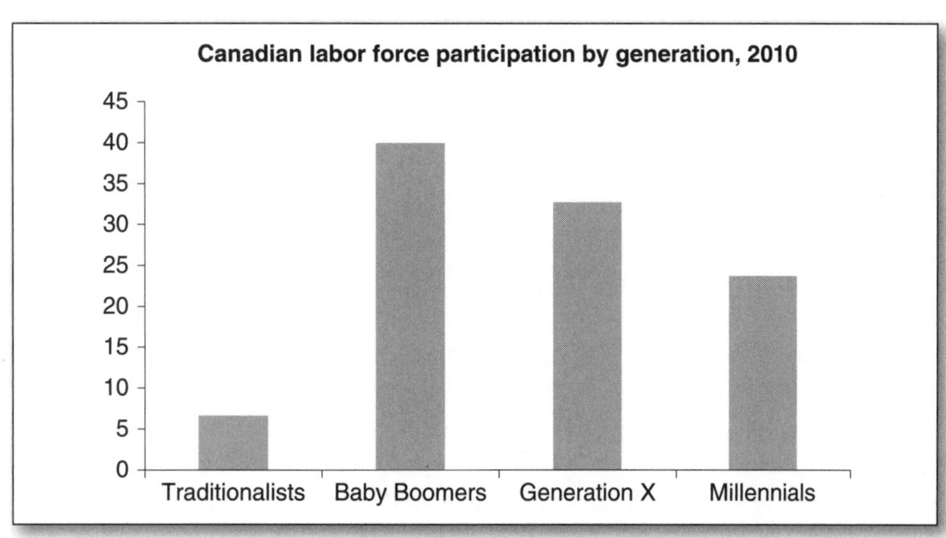

Source: Statistics Canada, "Table 282–0001: Labour Force Characteristics by Sex and Detailed Age Group, Unadjusted for Seasonality, Monthly (Persons x 1,000)," Labour Force Survey (May 2012).

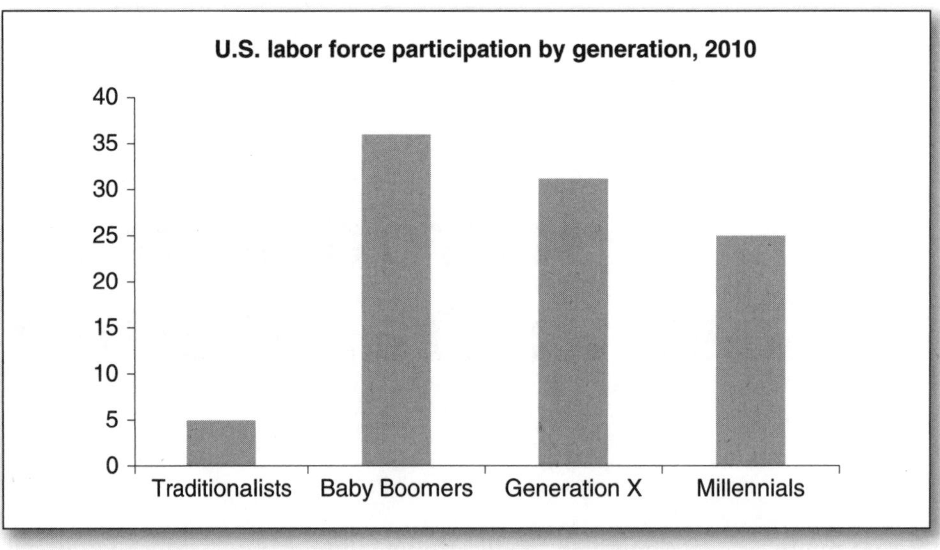

Source: Bureau of Labor Statistics, "Household Data, Not Seasonally Adjusted: Table A-13: Employment Status of the Civilian Noninstitutional Population by Age, Sex, and Race" (2012).

When you think of how difficult it sometimes was to translate between yourself and your parents, you can understand why one study found that 60% of people say they've experienced "intergenerational tension" at work (NAS Recruitment Communications, 2006). We think the other 40% either were not telling the whole truth or couldn't remember.

This book is meant to help you understand what it means to have four generations together in the workplace and also how to improve understanding so that when you have those generational moments, you can recognize and laugh at them. Otherwise, you might be left bewildered, frustrated, and sometimes angry.

This work is not about nostalgia or self-help. Recognizing the differences among the generations is meant to improve collaboration and deepen our understanding of how—why—others choose to approach a situation in a certain way.

Generational differences can cause the following problems:

- Questions of fairness
- Lower morale
- Problems working in teams
- Decreased efficiency/lower productivity
- Communication snafus
- Increased turnover and hiring challenges
- Gaps in succession planning

These are a few of the stories we've heard from educators just in the last couple of years.

A beginning-teacher support program director said:

> *I've been working with coaches in their 30s and 40s in our new-teacher support consortium and it seems all they want is a "list." What do they need to do with their coachers? How many times do they have to meet?*

> *Which pieces of paper do they need to fill out? They don't seem to understand that working with a new teacher is a process, that they might spend more time in the fall and less in the winter. They don't seem to get the big picture. They just want the boxes to check off.*

A 40-ish teacher said:

> *I get so many e-mails every day that I'm not even sure have to do with me. Everyone needs to be "in the loop" about every little decision. I am actually embarrassed by what people are putting in some of them. When did it become OK to just put things out there without going to talk to the person? And if I'm not making the decision, just let me know the final choice.*

A district office administrator said:

> *I know my most senior colleagues don't want to deal with this too directly because I can imagine it feels too painful, but we don't have a succession planning strategy in place and the majority of us are retiring in the next five years. I have heard comments like, "With who I am seeing coming up in the ranks, thank goodness I am one of the first to go. They just don't have the same work ethic. It'd be too hard to show them the ropes." But it is urgent. We don't have a deep bench. There isn't anyone in the pipeline. Who will take over? This is much more urgent than others realize. How do I explain to those "above me" that we need to put some time and monies into getting some positions designed so new administrators can learn on the job and be ready when we retire?*

If you're still not convinced generational changes may be significant, here are a few facts:

- In 1980, nearly as many (state government) employees were younger than 30, as older than 50, and of managers, 7% were older than 60, 16% were older than 55, and 28% were older than 50. In 2006, there were four times as many over-50s as employees younger than 30, and of managers, 9% were older than 60, 26% were older than 55, and *47% were older than 50* (Lewis & Cho, 2011).
- The U.S. Bureau of Labor Statistics found nearly one-fifth of the national workforce was 55 and older, the highest proportion since the data began to be recorded in 1948, while the proportion of young people age 16 to 24 in the workforce was the lowest since 1949—14% (Pew Research Center, 2009).
- In the 1980s, employees knew three-fourths of what they needed to in order to do a good job. They looked up what they didn't know in manuals or at the library. In 2008, according to research by Robert Kelley, we know only about 10% of what we need to know to perform well and need to find the remainder in some way, often using the Internet on mobile devices.

Who we work with and how we work has undergone dramatic shifts in a relatively short time. And we need not only to recognize it but also to capitalize on it.

A CAVEAT

We are painting with a wide brush when we talk about generations. We recognize that everyone is different and that each individual's unique circumstances tweak that person's view of the world. Our identification with our race, class, region, religion, sexual orientation, political affiliation, and more also influence who we are and how we work.

So when you read about your generation, you're looking at an overall picture, not a self-portrait. We're not holding up a mirror for you to see yourself but a landscape that shows what characteristics certain groups have in common.

In some sessions on being generationally savvy, very religious 30-somethings say they connect more to Traditionalists' values than the Gen Xers'. Some who have been raised by grandparents say the same thing.

Yet those born during a particular span of years were affected by significant social and cultural events at pivotal points in their lives that become the touchstones of the generation, the "where were you when . . . " moments. These are large-scale, such as D-Day, John F. Kennedy's assassination, the space shuttle *Challenger's* crash, 9/11. They are social, such as rock-and-roll or rap. And, of course, we're offering the North American view, as these examples show. (Jennifer's global work with international schools, however, shows that the generational filter is impacting work in schools everywhere.)

So let's "rent" the generational filter for now and see how it might impact our day-to-day communications in the workplace.

HOW TO USE THE BOOK

The book is divided loosely into two sections. In the first section, Chapters 1 through 4, we set the stage for understanding. The second section, Chapters 5 through 7, is aimed more at leadership and action planning.

First, we define the generations and describe their characteristics in Chapter 1 to help you get a sense of what holds other generations together. Who are the four generations currently working in our schools? What are their beliefs, values, and expectations? You can use this chapter to explore your own identity and to begin to understand the differences between your generation and others.

Chapter 2 begins to delve into how the differences translate into attitudes toward work and coworkers—beginning to explore the question, What difference does it make? We discuss how the generations view authority, seek validation, relate to a team, and differ in their needs and wants. We outline some of the challenges and advantages of working with individuals from a particular generation.

In Chapter 3, we begin to identify more specifically the widening gap between generations as we discuss how etiquette has changed and the new techtiquette, trying to help you build rapport by becoming more generationally savvy in interpersonal dealings with colleagues.

Chapter 4 adds to the bridge, we hope, with a discussion of communication styles. Again, the work is presented in broad terms. Individuals have more or less skill, or pay more or less attention to communicating, maybe, than the descriptions of the generation as a whole.

Groups of colleagues can use the first four chapters as a unit to explore and strengthen the workplace culture. The three chapters that follow deepen our look at the generations but with a longer-term and more systemic view. This section focuses more on workplace challenges for leaders.

The impact of taking a generational view of recruitment and retention is the subject of Chapter 5. With so many new administrators and teacher leaders coming into positions of influence and leadership, human resources now is a talent development resource.

Chapter 6 looks at differentiating professional learning for generational cohorts. We consider new teachers' needs, particularly, since the next few years will bring in more Millennials.

Lastly, we consider succession planning in Chapter 7. What should new and experienced teachers and administrators do to support the next generations who ultimately will be taking over their place in schools? How do leaders identify needs and plan for succession?

Each chapter offers activities to use with your colleagues to help improve how you collaborate. You may decide to use one activity rather than another, to begin with an activity and then use the text, or to read the book and then use a few activities. One chapter may meet a specific need. The basis for understanding generational differences, however, is always the starting point for improving how we work together, which ultimately improves our ability to meet our purpose—educating students.

1 Defining the Generations

Now that we have the background on the historic fact of having four generations at work together, let's take a look at the characteristics of each.

First we have to ask, What is a generation?

Our best definition is that a generation is "an identifiable group that shares birth years, age, location, and significant life events at critical developmental stages" (Tolbize, 2008). Members of a generation share experiences that influence their thoughts, values, behaviors, and reactions. Individuals, of course, bring their own personalities, influences, and particular backgrounds from their race, class, gender, region, family, religion and more, but some broad generalizations are possible about those born in approximately the same years.

One important caveat in using a generational lens is that a precise definition of each generation does not exist. There is no single authority that says that Baby Boomers were born in the years 1946 to 1964. In fact, for example, some break the generation at 1960 and others even earlier, defining those born in a span of late 1950s to early 1960s as the "Jones Generation," with its own unique set of characteristics.

Although sources vary the *exact* start and end years, and at times overlap a few years to allow those on the cusp of a generation to decide for themselves which they feel a greater affinity for, we have gone with a general consensus of the time span for each generation and chosen not to overlap.

In general, we believe, each of us shares a history and common experiences with members of a generation, and that collective consciousness creates our worldview.

The four generations are outlined in the following sections.

TRADITIONALISTS 1922–1943

These elder statesmen and women who work in our schools have been with us in the profession the longest. And given their inclination to stay with one profession, you might find them retiring with 35 or more years in the field—dedication that might shock the Millennials. This generation has seen world wars, an economic depression, and a slew of technological changes in their lifetime.

Traditionalists are:

Loyal

If you attend retirement parties and hear the number of years a Traditionalist has been with the same district or school, or has taught the same grade level, you will likely hear decades. Given an upbringing that had the specter of the Great Depression hanging over them, Traditionalists are content to stay put and soldier through the hard times. They may have not had the economic capacity or the will to move far from home, and they transfer that loyalty to their workplace and profession.

Respectful of Authority

They came of age in an era of traditional authority, and they welcome the recognition they feel they have earned; they may want to be called "Ma'am" or "Sir." They have always respected hierarchy and feel that, regardless of the individual, position has its due. They honor the roles others play and acknowledge them with formal language and gestures: handshakes and thank-you notes, punctuality and salutations all have an important place in their view. This emphasis on formal manners and traditions is not just generated by age. Boomers, when they arrive at a later life stage, may not expect to be addressed with a Mr. or Mrs. and be more open to being on a first-name basis with everyone from the grocery clerk to the doctor.

Jennifer had a superintendent from this generation that had a very Traditionalist way of handling issues that arose in meetings. When she noticed something occurring on the other side of the room that she disliked, she would quietly move to the individual and have a hushed moment of conversation rather than calling attention to the problem from the front of the room. As a Gen Xer, Jennifer might think nothing of just calling over, not uncomfortable in the least to speak up more loudly and address the issue from another side of the room.

Expect Delayed Rewards

This group paid its dues, worked hard, understood what it meant to move up on the salary schedule, sit in all the chairs before expecting a promotion, and do what they call "The Right Thing." This isn't a group that imagined stepping over rungs of the career ladder was possible, never mind jumping to the next ladder. Experience matters to them. In their view, you wait your turn and you are rewarded.

Uncomfortable With Conflict

Traditionalists deal with conflict behind closed doors. When someone asks a pointed question of a Traditionalist in an open, town hall-style meeting, we can imagine the Traditionalist answering, "Why don't we set up an appointment to talk about that?" Traditionalists don't tend to share openly in large groups and are more conservative in their style. They look at the information some younger generations share so freely on Facebook and shake their heads at the perceived immodesty of it all.

Thorough and Hardworking

Traditionalists often comment on what they see as a change in the younger generations' "integrity" and "responsibility." Traditionalists are concerned about giving the right impression and putting effort into getting a job done well. They might say, "If something's worth doing, it's worth doing right," as well as "Waste not, want not." They lived the expression, "Use it up, wear it out. Make it do, or do without." They are all about punctuality and penmanship.

BABY BOOMERS 1944–1964

This generation is represented by teachers with the most seniority who are anchors of the school, holding together their grade levels and providing institutional knowledge. They may be experienced principals or have moved to the district office, where they have been leading for the last decade or more. They are the most celebrated generation, largely because the generation is so large.

Baby Boomers are:

Optimistic

This group remembers when Kennedy was elected and Martin Luther King brought his message of social justice to the world. In a critical developmental stage, they saw a man land on the moon. They saw that individuals could bring about change as they witnessed the era of Civil Rights, women's rights, and peaceful war protests. Their idea of what the world is and can be was cemented by a sense of optimism and the idea that they could make a difference. They were there for "I have a dream."

Team-Oriented

With 80 million peers in their group, more or less, Boomers cut their teeth on the idea of "team." Coming together as activists and community members, they created the Key Club and Parent Teacher Association, Little Leagues and block parties, happy hours, and Secret Santa. They marched, they wrote editorials, and they pushed for change for the whole. They cheered each other on as they learned to use consensus as a tool. Boomers remember the teachers union in its heyday.

Here's what one Boomer said, seeing Gen-X teachers in his school making demands he wouldn't dream of and Millennials asking for promotions with minimal experience: "We just trudge along following and enforcing the rules and regulations. Our out-of-school lives are quite limited. We put in the extra hours and give stability to the department. We're the first to arrive and the last to leave. We're cynical, yet we're the most loyal to the school" (Martin & Tulgan, 2006, p. 27).

Service-Oriented

Boomers are willing to go the extra mile—to supervise the group on a Saturday, drive up to the state capital on a Sunday evening, go on the Washington trip, or get soaked at the school car wash fundraiser. They staff the booth and give directions in the parking lot. In addition to doing the job, they volunteer at home in their communities and in national organizations like the International Reading Association or the National Council of Teachers of English. They give back. A quote that defined their day was, "Ask not what your country can do for you. Ask what you can do for your country."

All About Process and Relationship

Boomers are interested in preserving relationship and getting results. They check in and network. They understand icebreakers, orientation meetings, get-to-know-you parties, and coming-to-consensus protocols. Boomers value the hallway hellos, celebrations of big events, and ceremonies honoring retirees. They respect rituals and community-building work. They won't jeopardize a relationship just to get the job done. Boomers are aware of macro- and micro-needs in a more foundational way.

GEN XERS 1965–1981

Born during the era of women's rights, the introduction of the birth control pill, and legalized abortion, they might be a smaller group compared with the generational groups on either side of them, but they leave an impression.

Xers are:

Cynical

Many Xers started to experience life after *Leave It to Beaver* in their own homes. Divorce became more common, drugs became more prevalent, and TV began showing a less idyllic side of the world. MTV, now celebrating its 30th anniversary, exposed Gen Xers to more skin and sex. Cable television began showing views from all over the globe, both opening Xers' minds to what could be and graphically showing what is. Used to being on their own from their latchkey days, Xers are ready to question authority.

Informal, Casual, Direct

Although Traditionalists had their work uniforms and suits, and female Boomers adapted with matching skirts and blazers, Gen Xers left the pantyhose behind. Their work wear introduced pantsuits and new protocols. They took casual Friday to casual every day. Xers don't rewrite the rules; they throw them away. Xers are less intimidated by authority and less interested in trying to be a part of it. Working groups became less hierarchical in response as communications flattened the traditional structure. Think of start-ups such as Google, Yahoo, and eBay, where workers are more entrepreneurial.

> One new Gen-X administrator caused some ripples among older generation coworkers when she regularly took Fridays or Mondays off to travel with her husband for his out-of-town bowling tournaments. In addition, she limited her hours in the building so she could be available to her extended family members. She worked hard while at work, but gave at least equal commitment to having a life outside of work.

Self-Reliant

Many Gen Xers have been accustomed most of their lives to being self-reliant, either through living with single parents or being latchkey kids with two parents working. They have a strong sense of autonomy. Gen Xers are more likely to want to work solo. They can be trusted to do what they said they'd do. They may not wear the team sweatshirt or join the committee, but they will get the work done.

San Francisco writer Ethan Watters (2003) coined the phrase "urban tribe" to describe Gen Xers' close relationships, and writes: "These may be the people you turn to to discuss the absurdities of the day, share confidences, help each other define goals, fall in and out of love, and schlep couches and big-screen TVs from one apartment to the next." For many Xers, friends become like family—a community and closest source of support.

Want Life/Work Balance

Gen Xers, perhaps a bit ungrateful to the Boomers who fought for union rights, women's rights, and civil rights, used their rights to create a better life-work balance. More than previous generations, Gen Xers want jobs, family, and friends—and will figure out how to blend their lives without becoming workaholics.

> For an idea of how you may compare with your youngest coworkers, try this quiz: http://pewresearch.org/millennials/quiz/index.php.

MILLENNIALS 1982–2000

The Millennials are the teachers and administrators who are around the age of 30 or under. As students, they benefited from all the research in the education field during the last several decades. They grew up with adults more focused on and aware of how to meet their needs instructionally as well as biologically and culturally. Although Boomers listened to radio through a single speaker or selected from three network television stations, this generation chose television programming among channels dedicated just to them (Nickelodeon, ABC Family, the CW, Cartoon Network). They rode around in cars bearing signs "Baby on Board" and had federally mandated individualized education plans. They will continue to expect the supports and structures they grew up with to be there for them in the schools in which they work.

Millennials are:

Confident and Assertive

In the media and at home, Millennials have been praised and pampered. They got trophies for participating on the intramural soccer team and a bumper sticker on the car to tell passersby that their parent was proud of having an honor student in the van. They have been videotaped, offered accolades, and publicly celebrated more than any other generation. Millennials believe that they are able to do it all—and their Facebook friends, magazines, and TV shows help bolster this belief, not to mention the businesses some of their peers have begun.

Accustomed to Praise, Supervision, and Structure

This group didn't go out to play kick the can in the street after school. With parents picking up milk cartons featuring missing children's faces, this generation was forced into scheduled clubs, groups, teams, activities, and lessons. Structured interaction became the norm. Free play was out, and play dates became another note on the schedule. Millennials are accustomed to structure and adult supervision.

> A new Millennial teacher worked excitedly to prepare her classroom with help from a few teachers in her grade level, her friends, neighbors, and her mother. She looked forward eagerly each week to her grade-level team meetings, and she regularly sought out her principal and others in her building for information and feedback. Alone in the classroom, though, she said she was overwhelmed by the "silence."

> One e-mentoring program a teacher participated in included a phone or Skype meeting at least once a week, along with additional e-groups with people doing the same job across the country. It was a great opportunity to receive support since she was in a rural town. Her supervisor suggested that many mentors texted and that, if she e-mailed or texted from her classroom when she needed help, she might get a quick response addressing her question. Used to immediate responses, the teacher found this program to be a natural fit.

Progressive, Globally Minded, and Open to Diverse Views

This generation has been exposed to more rapid social change and a changing demographic in the nation. They are accepting of others who are not like them, shrugging off differences that caused riots in earlier generations. With the globalized economy and instant communications that connect people around the world, they view the world in the same way that Boomers once may have viewed the nation—a bit large, but easily navigable.

Able to Multitask

No matter what more recent research has to say about human capacity to multitask, this generation believes it can. They grew up watching television, doing homework, and talking to friends at the same time. They believe they can continue their own education, hold down a job, and have a social life—all at the same time. They are completely at home with technology and able to adapt to the latest innovations intuitively, without an instruction manual. Technology is a background element of whatever task is at hand. They play their iPod while instant chatting on Facebook as they answer texts on their cell while writing a lesson plan based on tweets that lead them to others' ideas on the Internet.

Less Prepared Than Other Generations to Handle Difficult Situations

Used to structure and authorities giving them instructions of what to do, people in this generation may be challenged by new tasks that require independence, resilience, and resourcefulness. Many in this generation have not been allowed to fail before, and the possibility is frightening.

What makes your generation unique?

Here's what the generations believe sets them apart.

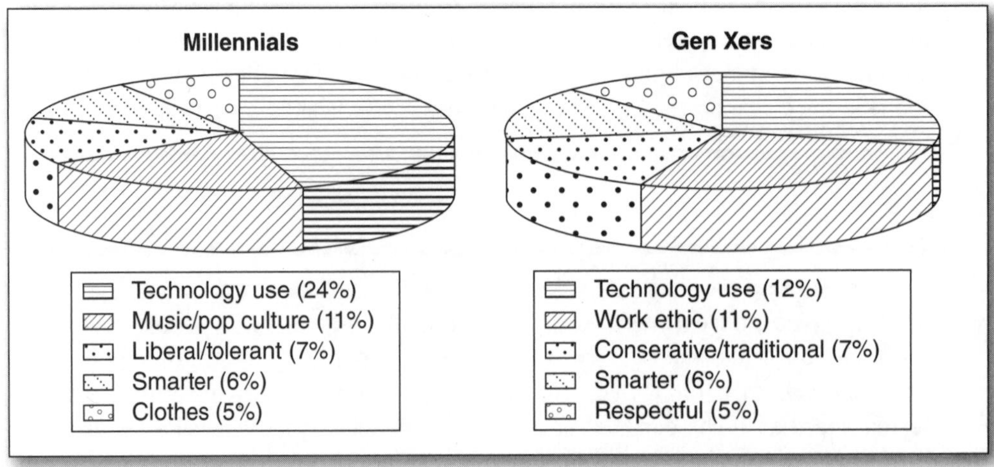

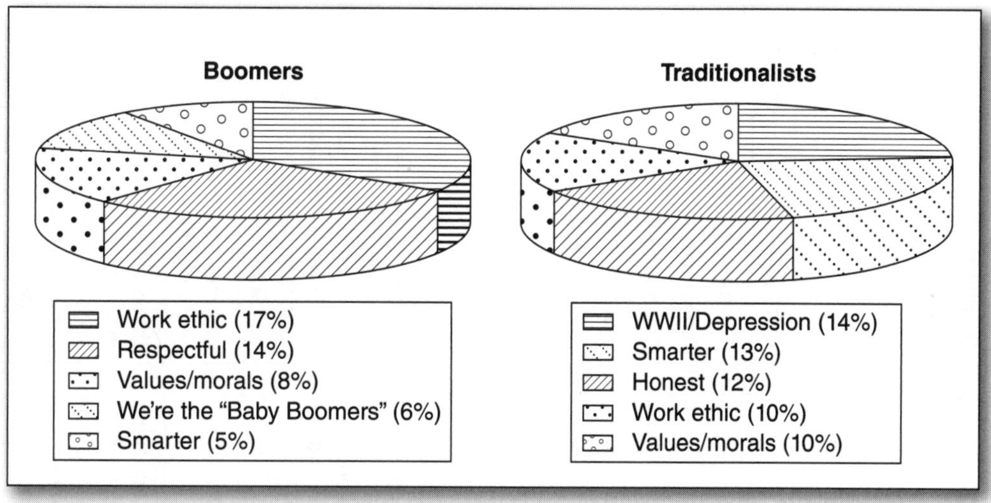

Source: Adapted from Pew Research Center (2010).

ACTIONS

It's time to identify the characteristics you relate to in your own generation, to see whether you now can recognize characteristics of other generations, and to process your learning. Use the activities in this chapter to make sense of what you have read.

CHAPTER 1 SUMMARY

	Traditionalists (1922–1943) 52–62 million	**Boomers (1944–1964) 80 million**	**Gen Xers (1965–1981) 50 million**	**Millennials (1982–2000) 70 million**
Other definitions	1922–1945 1930–1945 1900–1945	1946–1964 1943–1960	1961–1980 1965–1976 1965–1977 1965–1980	1977–1990 1977–2000 1980–2000 1981–1999 1981–2000
Other names	Veterans Radio Babies Silent Generation Matures Traditionals The Greatest Generation	Baby Boomers The "ME" Generation	Baby Busters Latchkey Kids	Baby Busters Echo Boomers Generation Y Generation Why Generation Next Nexters Internet Generation iGeneration Mosaics
Characteristics	Patriotic, loyal, respectful of authority, formal, hierarchical, dedicated, risk-averse, detail-oriented, hard working, financially and socially conservative	Optimistic, idealistic, educated, competitive, diplomatic, loyal, high expectations, opinionated	Skeptical, resourceful, independent, entrepreneurial, pragmatic, straightforward	Technologically savvy, empowered, pragmatic, confident, collaborative, neotraditionalist, community-centered, versatile, very busy
Need	Respect, commitment, consistency, privacy	Privacy, validation	Flexibility, work-life balance	Fast rewards, instant feedback, sense of safety
General description	Their name says it all. They didn't redefine the nation's values—they just did their job of winning World War II. They are patriotic, civic-minded, frugal, and private. They	Growing up in a time of economic prosperity, they could afford to focus on their own goals and achievement. They are willing to sacrifice for success and	Less optimistic than Boomers, they were highly criticized as slackers. Their cynicism is born of witnessing corruption revealed and changing values.	This is a generation of multitaskers who value flexibility and freedom. They are socially conscious, highly educated, and tolerant of authority, having been

	Traditionalists **(1922–1943)** **52–62 million**	**Boomers** **(1944–1964)** **80 million**	**Gen Xers** **(1965–1981)** **50 million**	**Millennials** **(1982–2000)** **70 million**
General description (continued)	may struggle with diversity, having grown up in mostly homogenous groups. Life often revolved around family, school, and church.	are often viewed as workaholics.	They are highly independent and less committed to any organization than to gaining job skills that will take them to their next job. They are unimpressed by titles and authority. They want a life/work balance and are willing to sacrifice to attain it.	coddled and scheduled by parents. They are more inclusive and accepting than prior generations as their world has been increasingly diverse. They are overwhelmingly confident, public in sharing information, and optimistic. They are adaptable, having grown up with constant change.
Defining events	Great Depression Pearl Harbor and World War II GI Bill Korean War	Cold War Civil Rights Act Rock and roll Assassinations of J.F.K., M.L.K. Woodstock Vietnam War Chappaquiddick Watergate Energy crisis	Computers *Challenger* space shuttle Fall of the Berlin Wall AIDS Oklahoma City O.J. Simpson Chernobyl International Space Station	Internet Diversity Columbine 9/11 Darfur
Technology	Automobiles more common Radio Magazines and newspapers Party telephone lines Handwritten letters	Color TV Car-sized computers in institutions Typewriters Landline telephones	Cable TV Video games MTV	1,000 TV channels Internet Cell phones Instant networking with peers Digital information at their fingertips

(Continued)

(Continued)

	Traditionalists **(1922–1943)** **52–62 million**	**Boomers** **(1944–1964)** **80 million**	**Gen Xers** **(1965–1981)** **50 million**	**Millennials** **(1982–2000)** **70 million**
Job prospects	Options often were limited by race, gender, and family background. Women's career options were severely limited, and few pursued higher education. Strong unions supported skilled trades and provided good livings for the working class. Work often resulted in tangible goods, rather than services.	Many individuals were expected to follow their parents' career paths. Good jobs could be had with a high school diploma and on-the-job training. Company loyalty could lead to lifetime employment. Midcareer, they found that retraining became necessary and layoffs were possible—and traumatic.	Factory and labor jobs began to disappear, and this generation became more technologically savvy. Telecommunications became a field, and technology gave rise to new industries.	Knowledge is power, and this generation knows it will need to develop its own expertise to compete economically. Work is less about producing goods than working with information.
Family life	More families had both father and stay-at-home mother. Mixed race families were rare. Divorce was difficult and uncommon.	More women joined the workforce rather than staying home to raise families.	Increase in divorce led to more single-parent families.	Typical families may be single parents, never-married biological parents, blended families, multiracial, multigenerational, or same-sex partner parents.
Organizational structures	A civic-minded generation that fought in World War II. The government has focused on them throughout their lives, from the GI bill through Social Security and Medicare, and they have a better attitude toward government as a result. They are hierarchical, with slower communications through bureaucratic processes.	Structures still surround the workplace, and technology begins to exert an influence. Machines begin to change the nature of work.	Globalization and free trade start to force organizations to restructure. A flatter system often results, and formal hierarchies are loosened. Many jobs, especially middle management, are outsourced overseas or eliminated.	Instant communication allows for much different work relationships, with rapidly changing norms and more unpredictability.
Heroes	Superman Joe DiMaggio Walter Cronkite John Wayne Franklin Delano Roosevelt	John Glenn Martin Luther King Jr.	Someone they seek out.	Danica Patrick Jennifer Hudson Josh Groban

	Traditionalists **(1922–1943)** **52–62 million**	**Boomers** **(1944–1964)** **80 million**	**Gen Xers** **(1965–1981)** **50 million**	**Millennials** **(1982–2000)** **70 million**
Pop icons	Wheaties Mickey Mouse The Lone Ranger	Slinkies TV dinners The peace sign Mood rings Bell bottoms Brooks Brothers	Brady Bunch E.T. Cabbage Patch Kids	Barney Oprah X Games
Literature	*Daily newspaper* *The Bible* *Gone With the Wind*	*Catcher in the Rye* *Atlas Shrugged* *Lord of the Rings* *MAD magazine*	*The Stand* *Angels and Demons* *Wired magazine*	*Harry Potter* *Video games*
TV shows	*The Lone Ranger, The Cisco Kid, The George Burns and Gracie Allen Show, The Abbott and Costello Show, The Roy Rogers Show, The Jack Benny Program*	*Laugh-In, What's My Line?, I Love Lucy, Bonanza, American Bandstand, The Twilight Zone, Looney Tunes, Tom and Jerry, Maverick, Doctor Who, Star Trek*	*Little House on the Prairie, Dallas, Saturday Night Live, M*A*S*H, The Muppet Show, The Waltons, The Six Million Dollar Man*	*The Simpsons, Saved By the Bell, Full House, Star Trek: The Next Generation, The Cosby Show, Seinfeld*

ACTIVITY 1

My Generation

Objective: To encourage participants to understand how different experiences in their upbringing can help them identify with a particular generation and to identify that generation.

Time: 15 minutes.

Materials: Pens or pencils, a copy of the questionnaire for each group member.

Directions:

Circle the answer that most closely represents your formative years. The answers are meant to be representative rather than comprehensive.

The technology I can't remember living without:

a. Radio

b. Color televisions

c. Pocket calculators, phone answering machines, video arcade, Sony Walkman, ATM, personal computer

d. Fax machine, IPod, e-mail, CD, GPS

The phrase that resonates the most with me is:

a. "And that's the way it is."

b. "What was your number?"

c. "Show me the money!"

d. "Tweet it."

The comedian I most remember is:

a. George Burns

b. Carol Burnett

c. Jason Alexander

d. Adam Sandler

Your beverage of choice might be:

a. Strong coffee, black

b. Coke

c. Half decaf, vanilla, no foam, extra hot grande latte

d. 5-Hour Energy

One of the most famous athletes as I was growing up was:

a. Babe Ruth

b. Jackie Robinson

c. Pete Rose

d. Michael Jordan

The historical event that most deeply affected me is expressed by this phrase:

a. "A chicken in every pot."—President Herbert Hoover
b. "The president is dead."—Walter Cronkite
c. "Mr. Gorbachev, tear down this wall."—President Ronald Reagan
d. "On nights like this one, we can say to those families who lost loved ones to al Qaeda's terror: Justice has been done."—President Barack Obama

When I was young, I played with:

a. Jacks, marbles
b. G.I. Joe, the Viewmaster
c. Pound Puppies, Rubik's Cube, Teenage Mutant Ninja Turtles, Transformers
d. Tomagachi, Polly Pocket, Care Bears

Which songs were popular as you were growing up?

a. "Boogie Woogie Bugle Boy," "Sentimental Journey"
b. "Homeward Bound," "Blowing in the Wind"
c. "We're Not Gonna Take It," "Don't You Forget About Me"
d. "Baby One More Time," "I Kissed a Girl"

Which show was a favorite of the kids of your generation?

a. The Shadow
b. Captain Kangaroo
c. Sesame Street
d. SpongeBob SquarePants

Which TV shows/characters did you relate to?

a. *The Honeymooners*
b. *Dennis the Menace, The Brady Bunch*
c. *Friends*
d. *Hannah Montana, Drake and Josh*

Which of these candies stocked the shelves when you were young?

a. Black Cow, Slo-Poke, Chick-o-Sticks, LifeSavers, Mallo Cups, Red Hots, Zagnuts
b. Atomic Fireballs, Candy Necklace, Pez, Wax Bottles
c. World's Largest Gummy Bear, Airheads, Banana Runts, Big League Chew, Nerds
d. Gobstoppers, Warheads, Hershey's Cookies'n' Creme

Add up the number of times you responded to each letter. If you have mostly As, you are a Traditionalist; mostly Bs, a Boomer; mostly Cs, a Gen Xer; and mostly Ds, a Millennial.

(For a Canadian version of this quiz, please go to www.jenniferabrams.com.)

ACTIVITY 2

Sounds of the Times

Objective: To help group members differentiate among the generations and understand the changes that have occurred in a relatively short period of history.

Time: 30 minutes, plus preparation time.

Materials: Computer with Internet access, tape recorder, paper, and pencils.

Directions:

1. In advance of the session, identify a facilitator who will review the article at www.npr.org/blogs/krulwich/2011/11/28/142859563/what-i-still-hear-sounds-that-have-disappeared?ps=cprs, which offers recordings of once-familiar sounds that will be recognizable by different generations. The facilitator then may choose to add to "sounds of a generation" using a tape recorder. The facilitator may use information from this book or seek out members of the generations to ask about familiar sounds.
2. As the group meets, play the sounds from the National Public Radio recording and/or the facilitator's collected sounds.
3. Ask participants to identify the sounds.
4. Share responses.
5. Discuss who identified the sounds and what changes have occurred in just a few generations.
6. Consider:
   - What are the implications of the changes in technology for generational differences at work?
   - What changes have most affected your generation?
   - How have these changes shaped the way your generation views the world?

ACTIVITY 3

Generational Characteristics

Objective: To create deeper understanding of the differences among generations and what each can contribute, and to help other generations become more aware of and understanding of differences.

Time: 30 to 45 minutes, depending on number of generations.

10 to 15 minutes for generational group work; 5 minutes for a gallery walk; 20 minutes for discussion.

Materials: Charting paper, markers, copies of the worksheet for each participant.

Directions:

1. Divide the group by generations. Allow individuals to select the generation with which they most identify based on reading the chapter.
2. Ask each group to designate a note taker. Ask each note taker to write the generation's name at the top of the chart page and to create three columns headed Characteristics, Values, and Contributions.
3. Ask each group to discuss and take notes in response to these questions:
   - What are the characteristics of your generation?
   - What do you value as a generation?
   - What does your generation contribute to our school/district?

Groups may refer to the summary chart in the chapter as a starting point for discussion. For example, Millennials might discuss characteristics in the chart and determine that they value opportunities to use technology. Boomers might find that they value the ability to work together to solve problems. Xers might discuss how their independence leads to innovations within the district.

4. Post the charts. Have participants do a gallery walk.
5. Give each participant a copy of the worksheet. Have generational groups discuss and take notes in response to these questions:
   - What are the characteristics of each generation?
   - What does the generation value?
   - What can you learn from the generation?
   - What can you teach the generation?
6. As a whole group, ask participants to report out responses from their worksheets. Encourage members to ask questions, share comments, and report on their own generation's views.
7. Ask the group:
   - What did you learn about another generation that was unexpected?
   - What gave you greater insight into another generation?
   - How might your response to a situation change based on what you now know or understand?
   - How might we use this information to change or adapt the way we do things to better use the skills and abilities of different generations?

WORKSHEET

	Characteristics	Values	Contributions
Traditionalists			
Baby Boomers			
Generation X			
Millennials			

ACTIVITY 4

Know the Four Generations

Objective: To begin to recognize the specific characteristics of different generations and deepen understanding that will lead to improved relationships.

Time: 45 to 60 minutes, depending on group size.

Materials: A copy of the worksheet for each participant, pens, or pencils.

Directions: Working individually or in small groups, depending on the group size, match the statement to the generation it describes. Compare answers with the answer key. Discuss the results that are different from the key and how those perceptions may affect working relationships.

Use these codes for your responses:

T—Traditionalist

B—Baby Boomer

X—Generation Xer

M—Millennial

1. They like consistency and uniformity.
2. They are confident.
3. They tend to be optimistic.
4. They are conformers.
5. They are skeptical.
6. They have a nontraditional orientation about time and space.
7. They are more comfortable with their parents' values and are more conventional than other generations.
8. Their spending style is conservative.
9. They believe in growth and expansion.
10. They are team-oriented.
11. Their approach to authority is casual.
12. They are used to being sheltered and being kept safe.
13. They are disciplined.
14. They have always believed in law and order.
15. They want balance.
16. They were the first to learn about teamwork both in school and at home.
17. They like informality.
18. They have searched their souls—repeatedly, obsessively, recreationally.

19. They are past-oriented and history-absorbed.
20. They feel pressured and pushed.
21. They are self-reliant.
22. They are high-achieving.
23. They have pursued their own personal gratification, uncompromisingly, and often at a high price to themselves and others.
24. They are seeking a sense of family.
25. They like things on a grander scale.
26. They think they are special.
27. They believe in logic, not magic.
28. They have always been cool.
29. They are attracted to the edge.
30. They think of themselves as stars of the show.

Discuss:

- Do you disagree with any of the statements about your own generation?
- How much do the statements about your generation reflect you individually?

Answers: 1. T; 2. M; 3. B; 4. T; 5. X; 6. X; 7. M; 8. T; 9. B; 10. M; 11. X; 12. M; 13. T; 14. T; 15. X; 16. B; 17. X; 18. B; 19. T; 20. M; 21. X; 22. M; 23. B; 24. X; 25. T; 26. M; 27. T; 28. B; 29. X; 30. B.

Working With Multiple Generations 2

Young workers often are ready to take on the workplace full throttle and may not stop to recognize the generations ahead of them.

In a survey of perceptions of their elders, subsequent generations responded increasingly negatively about older workers'

- Ability to serve as mentors
- Reliability
- Productivity
- Adaptability to new technology
- Interest in training
- Flexibility

Source: James, Swanberg, & McKechnie, 2007

These types of generational "rubs" happen often, and to avoid communication traps in the workplace, we first have to eliminate negative and false stereotypes about the generations. Learning the characteristics of each generation is a start, and looking at how the interests and values of a generation compare and contrast around workplace values can help smooth some of the friction and help us appreciate the insights and perspectives of those we work with.

Each generation has different views on work, ways of communicating, views on policies and procedures, approaches to working collaboratively, and career advancement expectations. This chapter will explore the different perspectives each generation brings in these five aspects of how we look at our work. Before you even begin to read this chapter, you might have some hunches of your own as to how the generations differ. If you're working in a group, you could choose to begin your work with this chapter with Activity 1. It might help you gain a better understanding of generational perspectives in your specific school or workplace and provide more context for the information to follow.

ATTITUDE TOWARD WORK

Veterans/Traditionalists

Take a long-term view

The movie *Restoration Road* has a memorable scene of men in dark suits all getting off the train, putting on their hats, and walking to work. It's easy to get the point that these men repeat this scene every morning—and do the same thing in reverse every evening. The message is that their work is a habit, a routine, consistent and continuous. We can imagine that we'd see the same thing five days a week, or more.

This generation expects staff to be at work early, stay late at the office, and demonstrate commitment to the job. They can't imagine what would be important enough for someone to leave a meeting early. They believe in taking on additional roles and sticking around for several years in the same position.

A Traditionalist colleague who just "retired" after 47 years said she was going to scale back and ease into retirement—by teaching 40% this coming year. Another colleague stayed at 40% and then 20% for years before she retired.

Boomers

Create change, but do it from within the system

As much as they might not want to admit it, Boomers who talked so much about The Man have become him. They've now risen through the ranks to become senior members of their departments or districts, or their county or state offices. Driven Boomers stepped on every rung on their way up the ladder, and their idea of work is that work is continuous. They expect to put in whatever hours are necessary—the work needs to get done. They often have a hard time with anyone who doesn't have the same priorities. They understand the work-life struggle and wanting to have it all, but find the balancing act difficult. If they are in management positions, Boomers have a job to focus on and want their colleagues to join in.

This generation expected to move mountains. They still do. However, they want to work in a team. They have learned that working with a group, they can bring about the changes they desire.

Xers

Balance work and life

Gen Xers want the opportunity to do a great job—but also to have a great life. They see work as one piece of the puzzle, not the full picture. They *choose*—or like to think they can.

Gen Xers seek autonomy to get their work done. If a family member needs to get to a doctor's appointment or if an Xer wants to run a marathon or day care isn't working out, they expect to take care of those personal details rather than sacrificing the needs of family to their job. Although previous generations might have felt pressured not to define "balance" too literally—or to see it as a consecutive rather than concurrent occurrence—some Gen Xers honor the life/work equation by spending less time at the office. It doesn't mean that those entrepreneurial Xers who are building up businesses aren't working hard; it is just that their workday won't look the same as other generations' 9-to-5 jobs.

With their tie-in to technology, they're perfectly comfortable blending work and lifestyle, so you may find them Skyping a different time zone before taking their kids to school, then leaving early from the office to train for a marathon.

Millennials

I will have many different jobs and careers, and why not?

There isn't a Millennial anywhere who hasn't heard that this generation should expect to have seven very different jobs in his or her life. Millennials expect to move up and on and to the side and over, to try different directions. They don't view any position as long-term, and they don't exhibit what older generations might call loyalty to a particular place or position. They're always impatient to see what else is available and where they might be able to go next.

Schools might understand that Millennials want to participate in the field in a variety of roles, but they may not be ready to accommodate the Millennials' wishes to explore, discover, and take on new challenges in ways that haven't yet been thought of.

COMMUNICATION STYLE

Traditionalists

Conflict avoidant, hushed tones

Traditionalists have always respected protocols. Ever vigilant around grammar, appropriate language, salutations, and greetings, this generation appreciates attention to detail. As conflict avoiders, they prefer quiet reminders behind closed doors rather than any open discussion or group remarks. One colleague noted that showing respect required her not to openly confront a peer, and she expected the same in return.

Boomers

Diplomatic, read-between-the-lines

Boomers are quite adept at balancing their activism with diplomatic language that helps move ideas along in the system. They might tactfully suggest, "Something to keep in mind is . . . " or "Just a thought for you as you move into the upcoming semester. . . . " Both comments have an open, suggestive tone, but listeners should note what's just below the surface and bring their own interpretation—understand what is meant, not just what is said. Not every generation can see or chooses to see the subtle, yet clear direction in the way a Boomer so diplomatically delivers a message.

Xers

Blunt, direct

For a generational group that introduced reality to TV, the concept of behind closed doors isn't the norm. Gen Xers yearn for transparent language. What do you want? What must I do? Because Xers are more direct, their tone may be misinterpreted. Xers may at times come across as dismissive and curt. Although they see themselves as getting down to business, others might see them as lacking interest in the big picture. They could be seen as undervaluing broader discussions around purpose and focusing only on immediacy and practicality. The "just tell me what to do" group really does challenge the other generations in communicating.

Millennials

Easy, clear, open, constant

Millennials want instant communication, short and sweet, clear and focused. They are the generation that moved from e-mails to 140-character tweets, from face-to-face to Facebook posts, from telephones to texts. They may be tongue-tied when confronted by in-person conversation as their social skills have revolved around communication through technology.

They need simple, authentic, and helpful interaction: Here is what we are doing. This is when we are doing it. You need to bring these items. Looking forward to seeing you! If you have questions, contact me in any of these three ways. Millennials prefer more just-in-time communications that still respect them, support their work, and help them grow.

RESPONSE TO POLICIES AND PROCEDURES

Traditionalists

Rule followers

Traditionalists play by the rules, save their sick days so they can accumulate the days toward retirement. They understand the reasons not to call in sick and have a sub on a Monday or a Friday, know what RSVP stands for and what they're supposed to do, and will fill out the paperwork for whatever the assignment would be. This generation has a genuine respect for protocols and a regard for policy.

Boomers

They wrote the book

As the older Boomers now form many of the old guard in the organization, they are the authors of policies and procedures, protocols, programs, strategic plans, forms, to-do lists and proposals. Boomers have shaped the structures and systems that make the schools run. They understand the state's timelines, the rationale for annual reviews, the way to write a state or federal report—from firsthand experience. They may not agree with the policy, but they will fill out the paperwork.

Xers

Rebels without a cause

Many Xers' immediate response to a policy is mistrust or annoyance. Required after-school assignments, changes in guidelines, new standards that need to be written for the annual review, a multipage dress code, required supervisory paperwork, changes to the report card—all are met with skepticism. The first word out of their mouth may be, "Why?"

The Xer response might be, "*Why* do we have to do this?" or "Is this just a top-down thing or is it really worth it?" An Xer might have to be sold on a decision before committing to it. As one Xer commented, "Explain why this is better and what this does that is different and more helpful, then I will do it." With an explanation, many Xers are far more open to going along with a request.

Millennials

Open to clear direction

Their own educations offered more details and direction, and Millennials continue to want expectations spelled out for them. Millennials have consistently worked with rubrics, continuums, checklists, samples and exemplars of different levels of work. They were tutored, accessed online support at any time of the day or night, and had parents who prompted them to turn in their homework after checking their online grade reports between midterms. Millennials will work with the system in front of them if the process is clear and what they are to do is spelled out. They want to access forms and registrations online, look for writeable PDFs, and are used to watching how-to videos on their computers. They may need a reminder—or two—but they are happy to participate in getting it done and even happier if it is easy to do so online.

RELATION TO TEAM

Traditionalists

"Ready to help, boss!"

This group is extremely agreeable—as long as everyone follows the rules. This generation claps when the boss arrives and shows up at required events. They are on time and able to complete the work without fuss or muss. They expect a smoothly run, politely attended team meeting.

Boomers

Relationships and results

This group invented team spirit. "System" makes sense to Boomers, and helping out and being a part of a process are very important to this group. They appreciate and use protocols and grids, processes and icebreakers to connect the group and value more than just individual contributions. They look for consensus, team-building activities, steering committees, and cabinets. They expect to have the big picture and head toward the goal with weekly team check-ins. The nuts-and-bolts meeting, celebratory lunches, retirement parties, and retreats all resonate with Boomers.

Xers

"Give me a checklist, and I will do it."

Xers are self-reliant, some might say to a fault. Their need for autonomy and independence sometimes gets in the way of their ability to "play well with others." Xers might be heard saying, "What do I need to do?" with an emphasis on the *I*. Xers aren't figuring out how to come together. Exchanging smiles in the hallway, greetings at the first event in August, thank-you notes—these are not an Xer's strong suit. Some Xers are seen as not being team players because they don't always view the team as being as effective as the individual.

Millennials

It's more fun with a team

Having been part of cooperative learning groups since elementary school, teaming is second nature for Millennials. They are used to sharing everything online. They are always prepared to offer a response or share their opinions in a very casual and immediate way. Their perspective is very non-hierarchical when it comes to group processes—everybody has a seat at the table, and anybody can contribute. So everyone else must be prepared for the Millennial's input.

CAREER ADVANCEMENT

Traditionalists

In due time

To a generation reared on duty and sacrifice, advancement must come only after many years of hard work and working within the hierarchy within the same organization.

Boomers

Pay your dues

Boomers believe sitting in all the seats for a requisite number of years yields wisdom. They set minimum numbers of years for teachers to become assistant principals, followed by several years as assistant before, in their opinion, someone has what it takes to be a principal. They may not require the same level of loyalty that Traditionalists do, but they definitely believe in paying your dues. They wouldn't have dreamed of applying for the lead job with just a few years of experience under their belts.

Xers

Merit matters

An Xer approaches career advancement as a recognition of skills and achievement, regardless of age or experience. An Xer might say, "If I did the thesis and have the credentials and background, what difference does it make if I did it in five instead of 10 years?"

Millennials

I can be anything I want to be

Millennials, often coddled by their parents and told they can do anything, see no reason to wait more than a couple of years before expecting to take a leadership role. Members of their generation have created startups and worked to solve world issues. They've received attention throughout their lives and the confidence they've gained from it carries forward in the workplace.

ACTIONS

It's time to find out how well you can see work from a different generation's perspective, helping you to bridge the understanding gap and possibly work together more effectively. First, review the information on the next few pages. Next, select activities for your team to process together.

ACROSS THE GENERATIONS: AT WORK

Challenges of Working With Millennials

They:

- Have difficulty accepting constructive criticism and often respond to situations emotionally.
- Need clear direction and supervision.
- Escalate common stresses into crises because they are unused to handling challenges on their own.
- Want instant rewards and gratification—and instant responses.
- Expect promotions with few years of work experience.
- Communicate using technology and are less comfortable with personal interaction.
- Expect work to adjust to *them* rather than adjusting to organizational needs.
- Don't follow the traditional chain of command and may leap over layers to get what they want.
- Are ready to share more personal information than others may want to know.

- Are very aware of their emotions but are less aware of others' and may take others' moods personally.
- Focus on their desired careers at the expense of their current careers.

Advantages of Working With Millennials

They:

- Have confidence that makes them ready to try something new.
- Will tell you what they're thinking.
- Were raised to work in groups.
- Care about what authority figures think.
- Can help others learn to use technology to work efficiently.
- Are globally and socially conscious.
- Are more inclusive and understanding of others.
- Value helping others.
- Multitask well.

Challenges of Working With Generation X

They:

- May be impatient—and show it.
- Have poor people skills.
- Tend to be cynical.

Advantages of Working With Generation X

They:

- Are adaptable.
- Have more technological literacy than older generations.
- Work independently.
- Are not intimidated by authority.
- Can be highly creative.

Challenges of Working With Baby Boomers

They:

- Hesitate to break out from the group or disagree with peers.
- Can be more self-focused.
- May put process ahead of results.

Advantages of Working With Baby Boomers

They:

- Are driven and willing to do whatever it takes.
- Want to please.

- Are team players.
- Form good relationships.

Challenges of Working With Traditionalists

They:

- Don't deal well with ambiguity.
- Are reluctant to question the system.
- Hesitate to speak up, even when they disagree.
- Are uncomfortable with conflict.

Advantages of Working With Traditionalists

They:

- Have a strong commitment to quality.
- Have good judgment, most often based on experience.
- Are less likely to change positions or seek outside opportunities.
- Come to work reliably.
- Are detail-oriented.
- Work hard.
- Are thorough.
- Are loyal.

Sources: American Association of Retired People (1995); Lipkin and Perrymore (2009).

GENERATIONAL VALUES

	Core Values	Goals	Assets	Liabilities
Traditionalists	Fiscally conservative Strong work ethic Sacrifice	To be respected To be valued	Stable Detail-oriented Thorough Loyal Hardworking	Uncomfortable with ambiguity and change Reluctant to buck the system Uncomfortable with conflict Reticent when they disagree
Boomers	Idealistic Focused on success Willing to work long hours	Lifelong learning	Service-oriented Driven Willing to go the extra mile Good at relationships Want to please Good team-players	Want to process differing viewpoints and come to consensus Reluctant to go against peers May put process ahead of results Sensitive to feedback
Xers	Entrepreneurial Ambitious Self-trusting	Independence No rules	Adaptable Technoliterate Independent Not intimidated by authority Creative	Impatient Poor people skills Inexperienced Perceived as cynical May have a hard time seeing others' perspectives
Millennials	Technologically savvy Eager to learn Confidence Work hours should be based on need and not overshadow personal time	To make a difference	Work collectively Optimistic Tenacious Heroic spirit Multitaskers Technologically savvy Capable	Need supervision and structure Inexperienced, particularly with difficult issues around people Challenged by in-person communication

Sources: Elliott (2009, p. 13); Zemke, Raines, and Filipczak (2000).

ACTIVITY 1

Generational Wordle

Objective: To understand one another's views about generational differences and discuss what stereotypes might exist, what the positive attributes are of each generation, and how some attributes might hinder optimal working relationships.

Time: 30 minutes prior to meeting; 45 minutes in group.

Materials: Computer with e-mail. Facilitator will need Internet access and print capabilities.

Directions:

1. Before meeting as a group, ask participants to read Chapter 2 independently and send a copy of the directions for this activity so the group can understand the objective before arriving at the meeting. After reading the chapter, each group member should write a short paragraph for EACH generation answering the following questions and e-mail the text to the facilitator:

    - Which generation are you writing about?
    - How would you describe this generation to someone who had no generational knowledge?
    - What characteristics have you directly observed in your coworkers of this generation?
    - What insights have you had about this generation? What are you noticing about those who are part of this generation?
    - What traits can you relate to about this generation that you find difficult to work with?

Group members should write in a continuous paragraph rather than answering each question separately.

2. The facilitator should provide a deadline for members to submit their reflections. After receiving everyone's input, the facilitator goes to www.wordle.net to generate a word cloud for each generation.
3. Adjust the word cloud with colors, fonts, etc. to make it as visually effective as possible. Print the word clouds in a format large enough for all group members to see in the meeting room, or print out a copy of the pages for each group member.
4. Post the Wordle pages for all to see in the meeting.
5. Discuss by generation:

    - What surprises you about our understanding of this generation?
    - What stands out?
    - What do you think may not be accurate in this picture?
    - What characteristics present the greatest challenges at work? How might other generations adapt with this understanding?
    - What are the greatest strengths we see in this picture?
    - What do you think might be changing about your understanding of this generation?

ACTIVITY 2

Who Said It?

Objective: To understand how different generations view work situations.

Time: 30 to 45 minutes, depending on group size.

Materials: A copy of the questionnaire for each participant, pencils.

Directions: Read each statement silently. See if you can determine what generation might have said what is quoted, and jot your response next to the statement.

Share your responses in small groups of three or four, and discuss why you think the statement was made by the generation you selected.

1. "I really want a job-share situation. I want to have time to be at home with my kids while they're young."
2. "I have a lot of great ideas, but no one is listening to me. They just don't like change around here. There are so many better ways we could be doing things."
3. "These new young teachers just don't understand the culture and the history. There's a reason we do things the way we do. If they'd just take the time to listen and learn, they'd understand."
4. "I'm putting in a lot of extra hours to do the best job I can possibly do. I don't get these people who pack it all in at 3 o'clock on the nose. They can't improve if they don't make the extra effort."
5. "I'd rather have the authority than have to listen to it."
6. "I want to be able to look back when I retire and say, 'I left a legacy.'"
7. "I want to hear more from the principal about how I'm doing. She comes into my room about once a week, but I don't really know what she's thinking."
8. "I just want to be given the project and then go do it. I don't need to have my hand held."
9. "I know I've only been teaching for two years, but I think I'd do a great job as lead teacher/coach."
10. "I think we all need to work much more collaboratively. I want to know what everyone thinks and feels about this before we make a final decision."
11. "*I* created this great kindergarten curriculum. I spent 10 years developing it. What do you mean I should give it to the other teacher? Let her do her own."

As a whole group, discuss:

- What emotional reactions do other generations have to these statements?
- Has understanding different generational viewpoints altered your reaction to the statement?
- What values and/or beliefs underlie the comments? How might we rephrase some comments to be more understanding of the other generation?

Answers: 1. Gen Xer; 2. Millennial; 3. Traditionalist; 4. Baby Boomer; 5. Gen Xer; 6. Traditionalist; 7. Millennial; 8. Gen Xer; 9. Millennial; 10. Traditionalist; 11. Boomer.

ACTIVITY 3

Generations at Work

Objective: To become more aware of current generational differences in the workplace.

Time: 30 minutes.

Materials: Copy of the questionnaire for each participant.

Directions: After reviewing the chapter, have group members take the quiz. Tally responses. As a group, review the answers and discuss the group's perceptions and the facts.

1. Which generation has the strongest preference for leisure time over work time?

   Traditionalists Boomers Gen Xers Millennials

2. Which generation has the strongest level of work satisfaction?

   Traditionalists Boomers Gen Xers Millennials

3. Which generation is most concerned about long work hours?

   Traditionalists Boomers Gen Xers Millennials

4. Which generation has the most difficulty accepting direction from a younger supervisor?

   Traditionalists Boomers Gen Xers Millennials

5. Which generation has the greatest proportion of college graduates?

   Traditionalists Boomers Gen Xers Millennials

6. What percentage of Millennial-age workers indicated they are likely to remain with the same employer for the duration of their working life?

   5% 17% 42% 69%

7. What percentage of Millennials aged 18 to 24 have a profile on a social networking site?

   96% 75% 54% 10%

8. At what age does the average person become "old"?

   30 60 70 74

9. Draw a line between the percentage and the generation that indicates it is important to "readily share knowledge with co-workers."

   Boomers 53%
   Gen Xers 69%
   Traditionalists 62%
   Millennials 69%

10. What proportion of employers in the general workforce train supervisors to manage multiple generations?

    1/5 1/12 2/5 1/2

11 Which generation is the most work-centric?

   Traditionalists Boomers Gen Xers Millennials

12. What percentage of human resource professionals said they were aware of intergenerational conflict in their organization?

    20% 40% 60% 80%

13. Which generation is the most likely to perceive *management skills* as important to workplace success?

    Traditionalists Boomers Gen Xers Millennials

14. Which generation is the most likely to perceive being *ethical* as important to workplace success?

    Traditionalists Boomers Gen Xers Millennials

15. Which generation is the most likely to perceive being *professional* as important to workplace success?

    Traditionalists Boomers Gen Xers Millennials

Answers

1. **Fact:** According to a 2012 Heldrich Center report, among those who had graduated from college and were employed full time, Gen Xers and Baby Boomers get more satisfaction from leisure than work by a margin of about 60 percent to 40 percent. Among Millennials in the workforce, however, leisure trumps work by a much larger margin of 68 percent to 31 percent (Zukin & Szeltner, 2012, p. 5; http://www.heldrich.rutgers.edu/sites/default/files/content/Net_Impact_Talent_Report.pdf).

2. **Fact:** According to a 2012 Heldrich Center report, Millennials who had graduated from college and were employed full time "are less satisfied with their jobs than either Gen Xers or Baby Boomers. Just 31 percent say they are 'very satisfied' with their job, compared to 39 percent of Xers and 44 percent of Boomers. And, while only about 15 percent of the older generations say they are dissatisfied with their job, one-quarter of Millennials are unhappy with their work life" (Zukin & Szeltner, 2012, p. 15; http://www.heldrich.rutgers.edu/sites/default/files/content/Net_Impact_Talent_Report.pdf).

3. **Fact:** According to a 2011 global survey of working adults, about two-fifths (39%) of younger workers (age 18–29) are frequently or nearly always concerned about their work-life balance, compared with about one in four workers aged 60 and older (24%). Nearly a third (31%) of younger workers also are concerned about pressure to work longer hours, compared with 17% of workers in their sixties (GfK Custom Research, 2011; http://www.gfknop.com/pressinfo/releases/singlearticles/007993/index.en.html).

4. **Fact:** According to a 2010 CareerBuilder survey of workers age 18 and older, "Sixteen percent of workers ages 25–34 said they find it difficult to take direction from a boss younger than them, while 13 percent of workers ages 35–44 said the same. Only 7 percent of workers ages 45–54 and 5 percent of workers ages 55 and up indicated they had difficulty taking direction from a younger boss" (CareerBuilder, 2010, para. 2; http://www.careerbuilder.com/share/aboutus/pressreleasesdetail.aspx?id=pr554&sd=2/17/2010&ed=12/31/2010&siteid=cbpr&sc_cmp1=cb_pr554_).

5. **Fact:** According to a 2010 Pew Research Center survey, "More than half of Millennials have at least some college education (54%), compared with 49% of Gen Xers, 36% of Boomers and 24% of the Silent generation when they were ages 18 to 28" (Pew Research Center, 2010a, p. 10; http://pewresearch.org/millennials/).

6. **Fact:** According to a 2010 Pew Research Center survey, "Nearly six-in-ten younger workers (57%) say it is not very likely or not likely at all that they will stay with their current employers for the remainder of their working life" (Pew Research Center, 2010b, p. 46). Among Gen-X workers, those numbers are virtually reversed: A 62% majority say it's likely they will never leave their current employer, while only 36% expect to someday be working for someone else. Baby Boomers, many of whom are at or approaching retirement age, are even more settled: 84% expect to remain with their current employer for the rest of their working life (p. 47; http://pewsocialtrends.org/assets/pdf/millennials-confident-connected-open-to-change.pdf).

7. **Fact:** According to a 2008 survey on Internet use, young people are much more likely than older adults to use social networks. Seventy-five percent of online adults aged 18–24 have a profile on a social network site, compared with 57% of those aged 25–34, 30% of those 35–44, 19% of those aged 45–54, 10% of 55–64 year olds, and 7% of those 65 and older (Lenhart, 2009; http://www.pewinternet.org/~/media//Files/Reports/2009/PIP_Adult_social_networking_data_memo_FINAL.pdf.pdf).

8. **Fact:** According to a 2009 Pew survey, "Survey respondents ages 18 to 29 believe that the average person becomes old at age 60. Middle-aged respondents put the threshold closer to 70, and respondents

ages 65 and above say that the average person does not become old until turning 74" (Taylor, Morin, Parker, & Wang, 2009, p. 2; http://www.pewsocialtrends.org/files/2010/10/Getting-Old-in-America.pdf).

9. **Fact:** In a 2008 survey of more than 2,000 U.S. employees, 69% of Baby Boomers rate as important the trait "readily shares knowledge with co-workers" and 71% report that the trait describes themselves. In contrast, 53% of Gen-Y employees rate that trait as important, and 56% feel that it describes themselves. Among Gen-X employees, the rates are 62% important and 63% describes themselves. Traditionalists have the highest rates on this trait, with 69% rating it as important and 83% reporting that it describes themselves (Randstad Work Solutions, 2008, p. 24, Figure 20; http://us.randstad.com/content/aboutrandstad/knowledge-center/employer-resources/World-of-Work-2008.pdf).

10. **Fact:** In a 2007 survey of human resource professionals, "Approximately 2 of every 5 (39.7%) of the employers stated that they train their supervisors on managing a multi-generational workforce" (Pitt-Catsouphes, Smyer, Matz-Costa, & Kane, 2007, p. 17; http://agingandwork.bc.edu/documents/RH04_NationalStudy_03–07_004.pdf).

11. **Fact:** According to a 2004 Families and Work Institute study, "Twenty-two percent of Boomers are work-centric, compared with 12 to 13 percent of other generations" (p. 7).

12. **Fact:** According to the 2003 Generational Differences Survey conducted by the Society for Human Resource Management, "Most human resource professionals (60%) said they were not aware of intergenerational conflict among employees at their organization, while 40% said they were aware of conflict" (p. 4).

However, the larger the organization, the more intergenerational conflict may come into play. Consider this:

Fact: According to the 2003 Generational Differences Survey conducted by the Society for Human Resource Management, 58% of human resource professionals from large (500-or-more employees) organizations were aware of instances of intergenerational conflict among employees at their organizations, compared to 34% of HR professionals at medium (100–499 employees) organizations and 31% of HR professionals at small (1–99 employees) organizations (p. 5, Figure 2).

13. **Fact:** In a 2007 survey of employees, 56% of Traditionalist workers and 54% of Baby Boomers perceived "Management Skills" to be an element of success in the workplace. In comparison, 45% of Generation-X and 28% of Generation-Y workers perceived Management Skills to be important for workplace success (Randstad Work Solutions, 2007, p. 17, Figure 12; http://us.randstad.com/content/aboutrandstad/knowledge-center/employer-resources/World-of-Work-2007.pdf).

14. **Fact:** In a 2007 survey of employees, 90% of Traditionalist workers rated being "ethical" as "extremely or very important" to workplace culture. In comparison, 84% of Baby Boomers, 83% of Generation-X workers, and 66% of Generation-Y workers agreed (Randstad Work Solutions, 2007, p. 31, Appendix Graph 25; http://us.randstad.com/content/aboutrandstad/knowledge-center/employer-resources/World-of-Work-2007.pdf).

15. **Fact:** In a 2007 survey of employees, 74% of Traditionalist workers and 70% of Baby Boomers rated being "Professional" as "extremely or very important" to workplace culture. In comparison, 63% of Generation-X workers and 48% of Generation-Y workers agreed (Randstad Work Solutions, 2007, p. 31, Appendix Graph 25; http://us.randstad.com/content/aboutrandstad/knowledge-center/employer-resources/World-of-Work-2007.pdf).

ACTIVITY 4

Relational Trust Across Generations: An Innovation Configuration Map

Objective: To understand what skills are needed to develop stronger intergenerational understanding in the workplace.

Time: Ongoing self-assessment.

Materials: A copy of the map.

Directions: Circle the description that best matches you in each row. In the row labeled *evidence,* note how you demonstrate that level. In the row labeled *reflection,* consider how you might improve your capabilities to move to the next level or to continue to hone your skills. In the row labeled *impact,* describe how you think your level of skills affects your work with colleagues. Revisit the map periodically to monitor your own progress.

	Level I	**Level II**	**Level III**	**Level IV**
	Able to define characteristics of various generations.	Has a general knowledge of some characteristics of different generations.	Recognizes that different generations are working together.	Has not thought about the relationship of different generations at work.
	Recognizes and honors coworkers' generational differences.	Is able to identify some characteristics of at least one coworker that may be related to the coworker's generation.	Understands that different generations are going to act differently, but may have stereotypical ideas.	Has not considered how generational influences affect people's attitudes and actions.
	Adapts communication style to meet different generational needs.	Is aware that different generations have different communication preferences (beyond technological) and sometimes targets communication to others' styles.	Is aware of generationally different communication styles (beyond technological) and occasionally attempts to vary communication.	Limits understanding of communication style differences between generations to technological differences (face-to-face versus texting) and does not adjust to meet others' styles.
	Differentiates professional learning to meet generational needs.	Understands that different generations have preferences regarding their professional learning.	Modifies professional learning strategies without generational awareness.	Offers professional development the same way it has always been done.

(Continued)

(Continued)

	Level I	**Level II**	**Level III**	**Level IV**
	Mentors or coaches with a clear understanding of the mentee's generational needs in terms of language, time frames for conversations, and technological needs. Spends more or less time on connection vs. to-do list as supports the mentee.	Mentor or coach understands and is aware of generational needs for mentoring individuals and often, but not consistently, meets those needs.	Recognizes that the mentee is from a different generation, but does not make accommodations for the generational difference.	Does not recognize any need to adapt the mentoring process for generational differences.
Evidence:				
Reflection:				
Impact:				

3 School Savvy Etiquette

A young, new superintendent wanted to encourage new relationships with key staff members, so he invited them to his house. Some of the older members arrived expecting hors d'oeuvres and cocktails. Instead, the superintendent was grilling in shorts in the backyard, with no shoes on. Each time the doorbell rang, he shouted from the backyard for the guest to "Just come on around." They helped themselves to drinks from a cooler of ice. The informality was reinforced when their new leader announced, "Geez, can you believe it? I'm the supe!"

The Amtrak conductor on the Midwest line was announcing the opening of the café car to passengers aboard the train. "The café car is in the rear of the train," he noted, then added, "Please keep your shoes on at all times when walking around the train."

Older generations—who assume that feet remained covered in public—might be bemused by both scenarios. Millennials, conversely, might have a hard time seeing anything to be uncomfortable about. Different generations have different social experiences and expectations. What's "common sense" or appropriate social etiquette to a Boomer may not be so for a Millennial.

Different generations have far different social experiences and expectations. They don't always share the same norms and protocols. If the question is "What does it mean to be a professional?" the answer is, "It depends on your generation." The bottom line in working together, however, is that etiquette really is all about making the people around you comfortable with your interactions with them.

So a few basic rules are always in order:

- Make eye contact.
- Be a good listener.
- Wait your turn to speak.
- Acknowledge when someone has spoken to you.
- Avoid negative body language.

After these basics, certain areas seem to be the main friction points among the generations. Getting clear around these areas allows everyone to be "two feet in the present'" and aware of schoolwide practices.

These etiquette pointers may be the start of a written document that all can look to as accepted practice. Jennifer has used this set of topics as fodder for conversation with schools at the start of the school year, in new teacher trainings, in work with new teacher coaches, and with professional learning team leads as discussion starters. For Millennials who want to know what the savvy thing to do is and for other generations who might not have had anything in writing about these practices, a list can be a good start.

TECHTIQUETTE

In one school district in Haslett, Michigan, a group of young teachers were friends and socialized. The teachers included both men and at least one young woman.

One night after the school year ended, the partying was heavy, a female teacher was passed out, and her colleague/friends wrote comments all over her body, some lewd.

Well, in this age of sharing, someone in the group also decided to take photos of the young woman. As social media will have happen, the photos somehow made the rounds—to students, to parents, to school administrators, and to the traditional media.

The teachers were not charged with any criminal acts, yet their behavior was outside the standards of their community, and they faced potential consequences not only administratively but in the opinions of parents and students with whom they then had to continue to work in a professional capacity. One teacher voluntarily resigned a coaching position.

The new ways in which technology infiltrates our lives call for savvier behaviors from each generation.

In a similar case recently with a young teen girl in Saratoga, California, the results were deadly. The girl whose body was defiled was so humiliated when photos were posted that she committed suicide.

Social Media

As the examples demonstrate, casual and unconsidered use of social media has real and very human consequences. Educators need to exercise caution on social media sites such as Facebook, YouTube, and so on. Students, parents—and potential employers—can and do check out pages and look at pictures that are posted.

Some teachers have been fired for their Facebook postings, raising questions of free speech, but not without lengthy battles.

Some general guidelines:

- Don't friend or follow current students on social media sites, including Facebook and Twitter.
- Be cautious about connecting on social media with parents of current students because of the possibility of perceived bias. Waiting until their student is out of your class shouldn't hurt a mature relationship.

- Don't post to social media sites during work hours.
- Never use technology at work to post.
- Avoid commenting about work on public media, particularly about students even in general terms.

One New Jersey teacher was fired after commenting in a Facebook post that she felt like "a warden for future criminals." Spoken, the comment might have been passed over rather than passed on. Online, such comments take on eternal life. Social media makes postings impossible to fully erase as they are put up on other sites unbeknownst to the author.

Check whether your district has a policy about friending, messaging, or texting students. As of 2012, Dayton (Ohio) Public Schools had banned such interactions.

Missouri initially passed a law restricting teachers from contacting students through private messages on any social media site before repealing the law and then passing a measure mandating that all school districts develop their own social media policies by March 2012.

Many districts are passing policies about general postings on social media. In Florida, one high school teacher of the year was suspended from the classroom and reassigned after posting—from his own home computer on his own time—comments about same-sex unions. In 2012, Orange County (Florida) Schools reminded employees that "private use of Internet and social networking is not private," and users should maintain their professional personas.

Bottom line: Follow your district's code of conduct, especially when using social media. If you don't have a code of conduct, consider creating one. Look to your state administrators association or local or state technology projects at departments of education for protocols.

E-mail

Addresses. Before we even discuss e-mail content, consider this a school savvy comment about choosing an e-mail address: Keep it professional. What e-mail address do you provide for personal use? What does that address say about you personally? The school district likely will provide a professional address to use with parents and colleagues through the system server. But you may hand out a private e-mail address for records, human resources, or some colleagues whom you may want to be able to reach you outside of work. Be aware of the impression you make to a current or potential employer, a parent, or anyone with whom you have a more limited, professional relationship.

Some (real) e-mail addresses we have seen lately begin with:

- Kinkykate
- 15cats
- glassgurl
- Bunnielove

Your personal address may allow you to reveal more about your inner self, but it may not help garner you the professional reputation you want. If you feel the need to express yourself descriptively for some audiences, consider setting up an alternate personal address that is less, well, personal.

Content. Find out the district's e-mail policy. Your district may limit what types of e-mails you can send through the district account. Be aware that legal precedent makes workplace e-mail and Internet access the property of the employer. In other words, you're not writing a letter in a sealed envelope. Your communications are open to viewing. In New Jersey, one teacher urging colleagues to join a political protest was found in violation of the district's e-mail usage policy and faced disciplinary action.

Consider this from the Medford (Massachusetts) Public Schools (2012):

"Don't put anything in an e-mail message that you wouldn't want posted on a bulletin board or used in a lawsuit or shared with the wrong person. Do use professional, courteous language that will not embarrass you later. People who may never meet you will be forming impressions about you based on the way you compose your e-mail messages. It's much easier to edit a message before you send it than to send an apology later."

Here are some tips on the *who* and *when* of e-mail:

- Reply within 24 hours, unless there are extenuating circumstances. Even then, a more immediate short reply explaining your unavailability is in order—acknowledge receiving the correspondence and indicate when you will be able to reply. Learn to use autoreply.
- If you need to RSVP to an event or a meeting in your district, do so within a day or two of receiving the e-mail.
- Be aware of the "reply all" button. You may be responding to everyone identified in the header—and others unknown who are listed in a blind carbon copy field. If you're not sure, simply hit reply (not reply all) and copy and paste recipients into the address field.
- Remember that anything you put in writing can be subpoenaed.
- If you have a strong feeling about an e-mail you have just received, write your response and save it to your draft folder. Wait 24 or 48 hours to reread it, depending on when you feel calmer about the situation. Ask a critical friend to read your response for tone. Edit, edit, edit.
- Always keep in mind who needs to know the information you are sharing. Should you cc: your supervisor, the principal, another administrator? Who needs to be "in the know"?
- Recognize that those in leadership positions—the principal, superintendent, department heads, mentors—are not your personal friends. Don't use the same tone and informality you would with your BFF. You may call your friends "dude," but some coworkers may not feel that friendly toward you.

Which leads us into more about the form of your e-mail content. Here are some tips on the *what* of your e-mail:

- Use punctuation. Capitalization in professional e-mails is also the norm. The audience *is* educators.

- Proof your writing to catch typos, wrong or missing words, and grammatical errors.
- Use clear subject lines. Do *not* put names, especially student names, in the header. If you receive an e-mail with a student's name in the subject, change it to "Your student" before you hit the reply button.
- Be careful of typing in all capital letters; some readers consider all capitals the equivalent of shouting. Use a colored or bolded font for emphasis instead.
- Begin with a greeting and reiterate the topic or question. The recipient might have forgotten the initial e-mail and be confused as to what a "yes" or "no" refers to. Try, "Hello . . . nice to hear from you . . . with regard to your invitation/concern/assignment. . . . "
- Less is more. Shorter is almost always better in e-mail exchanges.
- Limit the number of topics. If you include multiple points, you may not get everything addressed in the response.
- If you receive an e-mail with multiple questions, respond in a colored or bolded font directly below each question.
- If your e-mail is lengthy or deals with multiple topics, consider whether e-mail is the best medium for communication. Voice or face-to-face interaction might be an easier, more efficient way to communicate in this instance.

Texting

Texting has become a common communication mode, and the etiquette around the newest communication form may not be written yet in Emily Post (an old-fashioned guide to manners).

A Traditionalist we know recently discovered texting. He took to it as a regular form of communication, texting thank-you notes and other routine information at random times during the workday. He didn't understand what younger generations intuitively know—texts are for questions or information prompts that you need or expect a response to, not information. If it's information, use e-mail.

A Boomer colleague, conversely, preferred to get an e-mail in advance to set up conversations. She did not like impromptu phone calls.

For colleagues you may need to have ongoing communication with, you might ask them how they prefer to be contacted—face, phone, e-mail, text.

Personal Media Players

Leave your ear buds out when you're at work and in social situations. You want to appear accessible and not like you're trying to tune out those around you.

DRESS CODE

Jennifer heard about a principal, who, at the start of the school year, gathered faculty members in a meeting. "Stand up and say, 'Hallelujah!'" she told them, raising her arms in the air. Faculty members imitated her, dutifully repeating, "Hallelujah." As their arms went up, the principal stopped them with a "Freeze!"

You can probably guess what came next. She asked them to look down. "If you can see any skin between the bottom of your shirt and the top of your pants, consider changing the way you dress for the classroom," she told them. "And if you receive an e-mail with 'Hallelujah' in the subject heading, you will know what I mean and what you need to do."

More parts of the anatomy are seeing the light of day, especially with the trend toward low-rise pants.

One principal had to explain to a younger employee that leggings are not the equivalent of pants. Another supervisor responded to the question: "Are bras required?" At least the woman asked the question.

Many Boomer women remember when pantyhose were not just a preference. In fact, some Southerners probably remember wearing pantyhose underneath their shorts for even a casual trip to the shopping mall.

While public schools could very well have a dress code for their students, a teacher dress code could be a contested item up for negotiation. With more critical issues such as health care premiums and class size on the table, most school districts aren't writing teacher dress codes.

Some tips to reduce potential issues around dress include the following:

- Ask directly if the district *or school* has a teacher dress code.
- Read the student dress code and, by all means, do not break it.

Visually survey what your colleagues are wearing—and go for a middle ground. Some regions are more comfortable with tattoos, earrings, and casual footwear than others. Blend with colleagues, not with students. If you have tattoos, consider what they are and whether to cover them.

Think about limiting the number of piercings that are visible to students. You may not need all six earrings in one ear while at work. Could your tongue ring remain in only when you're going out, rather than at school? In general, despite the fact that the footwear showed up at a White House reception, flip-flops are not work attire. Conversely, wearing suits every day in an environment where khakis and a polo shirt are the common dress isn't going to help you.

Children and Pets at Work

For some Xers or Millennials with young children, day care is a challenge. Extended family members may not be nearby, and after-school meetings can be an issue. The obligations continue, but the set-up for childcare isn't always there. Although you may feel able to concentrate and more ready to work when your child(ren) are on site, that feeling may not extend to those around you.

A high school band director has two young children. His wife, who works in the evenings, is not available to be with the children. Because he, too, often has evening rehearsals, concerts, or other school-related activities, he brings the children with him and considers them a part of his extended band family.

High school band members and occasionally an available community member babysit in the back of the room.

Although Boomers and Traditionalists might react strongly and think, "Hire a babysitter," Gen Xers are more likely to blend work and family life. The context of the community also plays a role.

Some trainers or facilitators have no problem with a child coloring in the back with a bunch of crackers to eat; others find it distracting. Some schools used to working with high-needs students regularly provide childcare for parents to come to school and extend the same consideration to staff.

For others, their pets are their children and they think nothing of bringing their canine companion in if they're working on a Saturday—or even their parrot (really).

Consider:

- Does your district or school have a policy for situations that call for educators to be at a meeting or professional development opportunity after regular hours?
- Does the district have a policy on animals in the building? Some districts restrict any pets because of student allergies.
- Discuss childcare ahead of time with those running the meeting, recognizing that bringing kids to work is not always an acceptable solution.

ABSENCES

Many Traditionalists consider it a point of honor to be able to say how many years they have gone without taking a sick day. When they retire, they often are able to leave the office months ahead of the official date by using their accumulated sick leave.

These days, younger teachers are using their sick days more often and using leave for a family vacation, to visit a boyfriend, or just to have a "me" day.

One Millennial hired in the fall shocked her administrator by announcing she was a bridesmaid in several of her friends' weddings and would need to be off on those Fridays in order to travel.

The generations' views of what constitutes sickness—whether it's a 104-degree temperature or emotional distress—have changed.

Some schools may not have written policies, but instead have strong cultural norms. Be sure to find out how and when one can use days off. For example, ask:

- Can a day off be used before or after a school vacation break?
- Is there an expectation that educators avoid being absent on Fridays and Mondays?
- Is there an informal understanding of what is reasonable for using a sick day?
- How do we notify others when we are ill?

These issues aren't an across-the-board understanding of protocol unless they are spelled out.

MEETINGS

A new teacher was having difficulty making connections with colleagues in her school. She was a friendly, outgoing Millennial. She'd graduated from a university often considered as having the best education school in the nation, so she didn't think her colleagues were unhappy with her teaching skills. In fact, she thought her students were doing well and that her classroom was organized and working effectively. Yet in meeting after meeting with her grade-level peers, her comments were met with silence or someone turned to a different topic.

When the young teacher finally asked her mentor if her perceptions were off base, her mentor agreed to intercede. The mentor, a respected veteran in the school, approached one of the teachers for a confidential talk.

The mentor then met with the Millennial to offer some advice. "You may do better to wait your turn to speak—listen first to what the experienced teachers have to say and offer your thoughts after. Be careful how you phrase your ideas. Instead of saying, 'It's really stupid the way we . . . ' try saying something like, 'I've been trying out a new way of doing this and I think we can improve how we approach . . . '

"Even though you are very knowledgeable," the mentor continued kindly, "others feel like they have paid their dues, put in their time, and deserve to be recognized as having the experience and authority to take precedence."

Deference isn't an immediate response for Millennials or Xers. Boomers and Traditionalists almost expect it.

When it comes to meetings, working across generations can be a point of friction. Consider these points of etiquette that are more universal:

- Be on time to all meetings; in fact, for many in the older generations, early *is* on time.
- Bring what you need for the meeting—whether it's filled-in paperwork, your own pen and paper, or suggestions.
- Pay attention. Those leading the meeting consider it a sign of respect. Doing crossword puzzles, grading papers, catching up on the news on your smartphone will be noticed—however surreptitious you think you are.
- You can text under the table, but people will still know—and many will consider it disrespectful.
- Put your cell phone on vibrate. *If* you need to answer the phone, say, "Just a minute" and walk out of the room to continue your conversation. Avoid talking as you make your way from the table to the door.
- Avoid whispered sidebars during the meeting, especially with disgruntled colleagues. Negative energy is a virus.
- If you will need to leave the meeting, try to let the leader know ahead of time so your departure is expected.
- Watch your body language—eye rolling, sighing, shouting out, or giggling.
- Apologize if you think someone perceived you as disrespectful.
- Try to compose yourself if your mood is stressed or angry, and explain if necessary, without going into every detail.

- If you are running the meeting, have an organized agenda and keep on track, ask people to adhere to norms, and expect to have to manage conflict.
- Remember that you are working with colleagues, not your best friends. Your language should reflect that relationship. Don't ask personal questions unless the other person brings it up.

Groups with ongoing relationships, such as learning teams, may want to consider these points as part of group norms and set them up as agreements.

WORKING WITH OFFICE/SUPPORT STAFF

The front office secretary may or may not have positional status in the school hierarchy, but veterans know she has positional power and can make or break your work life. Want an appointment with the principal? Need help from the maintenance crew? Need to find a place for your team to meet? Need the scoop on a parent who's coming to see you? The people in this position are the heart of a building.

The same thing is true for custodial staff. When the light in your room won't stop blinking or a child throws up on the rug, their goodwill helps expedite matters that can be important to your routine.

We heard one story that really pointed to how important it is for young workers to understand working relationships. A new teacher, who had grown up watching her working mother interact with a secretary, had an impression that all secretaries make personal appointments. One day, she approached the elementary school secretary and asked her to make an appointment for the teacher to get a manicure. The request was not well received.

Courtesy should be common. Noncertificated staff play a vital role in school operations.

- Do not condescend to them or treat them as your assistants.
- Say hello to the office staff when you come into the office. Make eye contact.
- Ask if it is a good time to review something you need or when they might have time to do so—their workflow may be different than yours.
- If you're requesting an item, to have something copied or to get something done, give explicit instructions for the task. Don't assume understanding.
- Be aware of school procedures. If all copying is done at 9 a.m., have your copying ready by then.
- Follow the proper channels. Do you need a supervisor's or front office administrator's approval to have a support staff member assist you?

- Consider priorities. You may need your light fixed and that is your priority. The custodial staff member may be on the way to clean up after a sick child in another room. Be considerate; people will get a sense quickly of who really needs a quick response when they indicate something is urgent.
- If you break something or take the last of it, let someone know so it can be restocked for the next person.
- Acknowledge everything they do for you. Be genuine in thanking them.
- If a request is not met or not completed properly, address it in an understanding, nonthreatening manner.

Learning From Year 1 Teachers

In spite of our best efforts to be polite, friction sometimes arises. Some thoughts about the etiquette around conflict are as follows:

- If you are struggling with something or someone, talk it through with a coach, the new teacher mentor at the school, or a trusted colleague. Do not tell everyone in the lunchroom. Do not tell parents about it when they come to pick up their children.
- If you are going into a difficult meeting with your supervisor or the principal, bring your coach or a trusted colleague if you can.
- Go to the source whenever possible.
- When you need to talk to someone, approach that person. Do not shout across the hallway or the quad.
- Don't send a note or email with an attachment stating only, "How about getting this done?" The impression isn't a good one.
- Avoid having that difficult discussion in front of students.
- Students don't need or want to know about your conflicts with others.
- When discussing events, try to be general rather than naming those involved.
- Remember, those you talk about today may be part of your team tomorrow.
- Exercise care and caution about the time and place for addressing delicate topics—before school, after school, during passing periods.

Source: New teachers in Palo Alto (California) School District, 2010.

Etiquette is the grease in the engine, the asphalt on the road that smoothes the way to better personal interactions with others in the workplace. Although we can choose those with whom we spend time outside of work, we have to make relationships work at school. By recognizing generational differences in approach and discussing norms, we can come to a greater understanding of what works—and how we can communicate better, the topic for Chapter 4.

ACTIVITY 1

Raise Your Hand

Objective: To begin to recognize the differences among generations' views of etiquette in a lighthearted way.

Time: 15 minutes.

Materials: A copy of the worksheet for a facilitator.

Directions:

1. Read each statement aloud, asking group members to raise their hands when they hear the response they agree with.
2. Allow group members to discuss and come to agreement on answers. Group members should be ready to discuss how their generational viewpoint informs their responses and to suggest common ground.

Questionnaire

1. RSVP means:
   a. It's a party!
   b. Let the host know if you can't make it.
   c. Let the host know whether you can or can't make it.
2. Your e-mail address ends in @aol.com. You're most likely a:
   a. Millennial.
   b. Gen Xer.
   c. Boomer.
3. Emily Post was:
   a. An arbiter of good manners.
   b. A former principal that everybody loved.
   c. A television talk show host.
4. You open your e-mail from a colleague and the salutation is "Dude!"
   a. You make a mental note to call your colleague aside and point out the lack of manners.
   b. You get irritated and have trouble reading the rest of the message.
   c. You don't see a problem here. In fact, you sign your return message "Dudette."
5. You have to set up a meeting with your small group.
   a. You text everyone to see when they're available.
   b. You send an e-mail with a link to a scheduling tool.
   c. You see everyone during the course of a day anyway, so you just ask.

6. You're scrolling education blogs online when you happen across one written by a colleague. The blog is full of details about situations in your school, although no names are attached.
   a. You feel that your privacy has been violated and vow to bring this up to the group.
   b. You think, "Wow! I wish I was blogging, too!"
   c. You review the school's policies and procedures to determine whether blogging information like this is against the rules.
7. You have a colleague who makes you feel bad whenever you work together.
   a. You write an e-mail to the person about the situation and copy your supervisor on it.
   b. You begin avoiding the person and try not to be in work groups with her.
   c. You call the person aside and explain your perception, asking her to help find ways that your relationship can feel more collegial.
8. Your daughter's dance school is selling pizza kits to raise money for an outing.
   a. You help your daughter solicit family and friends and keep the form at home.
   b. You bring the fundraising form to work and post it in the teachers lounge.
   c. You send your daughter in to work one day and have her sell kits to the entire department.
9. It's 4 p.m., the end of the contract day, and the staff meeting is still going.
   a. You look at your watch and pointedly pack your things in case the principal hasn't noticed the time.
   b. You leave—your workday is done and you have things to do at home.
   c. You don't even notice the time; there's work to be done and you'll be there to do it.
10. Your group has been pretty down lately.
   a. You suggest a party at your place.
   b. You propose that the team dig a little deeper into what members can do to improve.
   c. You urge everyone to get some down time.

- Discuss your answers as a group. Which generations were more likely to choose which responses? What does that tell you about the generational viewpoints?
- For an added challenge, in pairs, try writing several questions of your own. Put on different generational lenses and see if you can foresee possible responses. Test your questions with the group.

ACTIVITY 2

Etiquette in the Workplace

Objective: To understand the different viewpoints among generations and openly discuss workplace norms of etiquette.

Time: 30 to 45 minutes, depending on group size.

Materials: A copy of the scenarios for each group member.

Directions:

1. Share a copy of the scenarios with each group member.
2. Working in small groups of two or three, read each scenario and discuss how different generations might view the situation.
3. Answer:
   - How would each generation be likely to react in this situation?
   - How might the other generations respond differently?
   - Should the situation be handled differently?
   - What is the most appropriate response in this situation for those involved?
4. Share thoughts and ideas with the large group.
5. As a group, discuss other situations that may have arisen in your own workplace. Share ideas about how generations might view the situation differently and the best common solution to create an environment comfortable for all.

- A student teacher is very technologically savvy. He has helped his mentor teacher considerably with new ways to use the digital whiteboard and with accessing Internet resources. The intern is continuously checking his smartphone for tweets and updates his social media site from the teacher's desk as his mentor teaches. When the mentor suggested that the intern turn off his phone, he put the ringtone on vibrate.
- The retired teacher has returned part time to coach new teachers at the school. She is knowledgeable and has decades of experience and wisdom to share. In fact, she taught with many of the staff currently at the school who all are comfortable with and like her. The new teachers respect her. One habit, however, is bothering them. The coach regularly looks over their lesson plans to provide feedback. She often turns back their papers to them with editing marks in red pen, circling grammar or spelling errors and typos.
- The central office administrator, dressed in a 1960s-style long, flowered, tiered skirt, sandals, and drawstring blouse, was explaining the state credentialing program to newly hired staff members. She presented slides and handouts of carefully outlined steps. This was a process of which she was particularly proud, since she had served as a member of the statewide committee that drafted the policies and procedures. As some new teachers began questioning the rationale behind specific steps, the administrator grew obviously more flustered. Some of the new teachers began to perceive her as defensive, even bordering on hostile.
- A new kindergarten teacher was very hands-on. She regularly could be seen working on the floor with children or kneeling or bending down beside them. Because the teacher wore pants that

tended to be the low-cut fashion, adults and children alike regularly got a full view of thong underwear as she worked. She also often declined to wear a bra. She told her friends she didn't think it showed and she was more comfortable without one.

- The mentor assigned to a first-year teacher was known for reaching even the most at-risk students and helping them to succeed. The new teacher was excited about what she might learn from this mentor. The mentor teacher began the year by setting up particular times she would meet with the new teacher and specified that she preferred e-mail communication between those meetings. The new teacher often had questions or situations that arose. She e-mailed the mentor regularly. The mentor replied as quickly as she could, sometimes within one or two days. She did not check her e-mail after 4 p.m., she explained, because she had responsibilities both to young children and aging parents.

ACTIVITY 3

Generational Norms

Objective: To come to a common set of workplace norms around matters of etiquette.

Time: 30 minutes.

Materials: A copy of the worksheet for each group member, pens, or pencils.

Directions:

1. Have each group member circle the answer to each question on the worksheet.
2. Divide into generations.
3. Average the response for each question.
4. Average the response from the whole group for each question.
5. Note how far generations differed from the mean. Discuss patterns: Where are the greatest differences? How do different generations define terms such as "personal information" or "formal"?
6. Work to create common ground.
7. Add statements if group members raise other issues that may be important to the group.
8. Form a set of written norms if the group deems it appropriate.

SCALE (1) Very important (2) Moderately important (3) Not very important (4) Unimportant

1. Colleagues should be dressed in business attire, i.e., skirt or slacks, nice shirt, dress shoes.
   1 2 3 4
2. Good opinions are based on experience.
   1 2 3 4
3. People in collaborative/professional groups wait their turns to speak.
   1 2 3 4
4. We should address one another more formally, with Ms., Mr., Mrs., or Miss.
   1 2 3 4
5. Tattoos and piercings must be covered up in professional settings.
   1 2 3 4
6. Everyone is on time to the meeting.
   1 2 3 4
7. No one texts, e-mails, or does outside work during the meeting.
   1 2 3 4
8. We use Standard English in our speech and avoid slang and swear words.
   1 2 3 4

9. We share information about our personal lives.

1 2 3 4

10. We don't shout, cry, or exhibit strong emotions in front of colleagues in the workplace.

1 2 3 4

11. We are well groomed.

1 2 3 4

12. We avoid discussing politics and religion at work.

1 2 3 4

13. We are able to bring our children to school when we have after-school meetings and can't arrange childcare.

1 2 3 4

14. We use our sick days only when we are extremely ill.

1 2 3 4

15. We avoid using personal days on Fridays and Mondays.

1 2 3 4

16. We can have our pets with us if it's after hours and we have to work late.

1 2 3 4

17. We don't post anything on social media websites that is outside the moral norms for our community.

1 2 3 4

18. We avoid borrowing supplies from one another except in rare circumstances.

1 2 3 4

19. We greet one another when we see each other in the morning using eye contact and a verbal greeting.

1 2 3 4

20. We use Standard English and spelling in our e-mails and written communications to one another.

1 2 3 4

21. We report it when we use the last of any supplies that the school provides so that the supplies can be reordered.

1 2 3 4

22. Our contact with students remains professional inside and outside of school.

1 2 3 4

23. We leave the workroom, staff lounge, shared classroom, or other shared space tidy.

1 2 3 4

ACTIVITY 4

School Savvy Considerations

Objective: To generate open discussion of generational differences around workplace norms and come to agreement on some matters of etiquette.

Time: Approximately 1 hour.

Materials: A copy of the worksheet for each group member, pens or pencils, and scratch paper for notes.

Directions:

Use these bullet points to generate group discussion around generational differences and the expected norms for your site with regard to each issue. An experienced facilitator should help to guide the discussion. Avoid references to any individual or specific situations to avoid personal conflict.

Ask group members to think about how a school might frame the norms around these topics. What needs to be put into writing? What doesn't? What other challenges have you noticed that you wish had been officially discussed or agreed to?

- *Boundaries with students*
    - Talking about students in front of other students
    - Talking with them appropriately in the hallways or on the campus
    - Talking to students about other teachers
    - Talking to students when they are disrespectful of other teachers
- *Boundaries with colleagues and parents*
    - Talking in the bathroom, the parking lot, the lunchroom
    - Talking in the grocery store, at a party, in the community
- *Classroom sharing*
    - Materials, space, cleanliness
- *Curriculum and materials*
    - Returning equipment (video cameras, calculators)
    - Using someone's personal property
    - Textbook sharing
    - Keeping things organized
- *Absences*
    - Leaving clear sub plans
    - Expectations of others covering classes for you
    - Personal days, sick days—How many? How often?
- *Thinking aloud in front of certain audiences*
    - Who is your ally? Your critical friend?
    - Who can you vent to? Cry in front of? Who can't you vent to?
    - Considering political beliefs, tolerance of others' points of view

- *Family and pets*
  - Bringing pets and children to work or meetings. Are policies in place?
  - What is legal?
  - What is appropriate?
- *Taking a leave or being released*
  - Sharing info about a leave/pregnancy/change of employment status
  - How to talk about it, with whom, and when
- *Categories for which one needs interpersonal and school savvy*
  - Time: What is late?
  - Space: Where is your space versus others? Interpersonal, classroom, etc.
  - Keeping your word: What is non-negotiable and required versus a maybe
  - Sharing personal information, such as family or medical issues
  - Emotional expression: What are the boundaries? Can you cry? Yell?
  - Manners/courtesy/noise levels: What is loud?
  - Food: Sharing it? Bringing it?
  - Language use: Are slang or swearing acceptable?
  - Hygiene

Communicate to Collaborate 4

A Gen-X parent arrived at her daughter's Back to School night after a long day in her own office, ready for the official presentations about what her sixth grader could expect in the coming year. Although she was used to the greater casualness of the West Coast compared with her native Midwest, she still was surprised when she took her seat in the science teacher's classroom and he stood in front of the parents to make his presentation in shorts.

"It was shocking to me" that he was wearing shorts, she said, "but not as shocking as his informing us that he was 'stoked' to be teaching at this school. I'm not sure what else I took from the 10-minute talk, but I did find myself wondering if this teacher was old enough to teach my daughter."

This parent's reaction was all about her generational lens. The phrase that stuck in her mind likely would have been passed over by her daughter—and by a number of the teacher's colleagues.

What we say, how and when we say it, the means of our communication—these things gave Ann Landers full-time employment for decades. With four generations now interacting as professionals in the workplace, however, the friction spots in communications have grown.

In most workplaces, when something goes wrong, we blame it on the "lack of communication." A BridgeWorks *Generations* survey (in Lancaster & Stillman, 2010) found that one-third of respondents said they often were offended at work by someone from another generation. Working together effectively in professional settings requires understanding *how* different generations communicate and how a message is communicated through the medium and our choice of language. Improving conversations among colleagues in schools is more than a nicety. Social relationships matter to staff performance—and therefore to student achievement.

WHAT WE SAY

Although some research says that 80% of our communication is nonverbal, language can still be an important piece of how we get along. Researchers are learning more about how words affect people physiologically—brain scans show the same patterns of hurt from harsh words as from physical blows. What we say matters.

Unkind words aren't the only friction point. The generations have changed what we are comfortable sharing. Millennials who grew up on Facebook and other social media sites posting photos of almost every conceivable moment of their lives often offer what seems to older generations like personal information overload.

Traditionalists may have been parents themselves in their early 20s. Today's 20-something Millennials often are more able to relate to their secondary school students than to their colleagues. The news is full of stories about young teachers caught in inappropriate relationships, making poor decisions outside the workplace, and sharing too much.

A young intern teacher recently blogged that she found herself attracted to one of her students and didn't know what she was going to do. She added caveats about his age being so close to hers. It was a straightforward "sharing" moment. The responses to the blog entry exploded.

Another teacher on a social media site regularly shares information about his panic disorder and the level of anxiety he has about going to school. Explaining to your boss that you can't come to work because you're having an anxiety attack translates, to a Boomer, into questions about your long-term fitness in relating to students.

Millennials share. Traditionalists and Boomers are more reserved in what they consider personal information for public consumption, and Gen Xers tend to be more interested in efficiency than in sharing.

Although swapping personal details can help build relationships, some topics that generations may not agree are meant for sharing in the workplace include the following:

- Details about weekend "adventures"
- Information about one's sex life
- Ongoing medical conditions
- Family problems
- Financial matters
- Political views
- Religious beliefs

Be aware of how other generations may view information. If you're not sure, talk with someone from a different generation outside of the workplace.

> A Millennial had just broken up with her boyfriend of many years and was heartbroken. She'd been picturing a future with this man—marriage, children, old age—and he turned out to be more interested in her best friend. When she called the school to explain that she would not be able to come to work for a few days, she was surprised by her Gen-Xer principal's "totally unsympathetic" reaction to her tearful explanation. Venting to a Boomer colleague, she found a less brusque but similar response.

Although we are focusing on verbal communication in this chapter, we want to acknowledge the power of the nonverbal. In one study, for example, researchers asked subjects to decide whether a tennis player was expressing the thrill of victory or the agony of defeat. Those who looked at the pictures of players at the decisive moment were remarkably accurate. But researchers wanted to know more, so they showed people the same photos—this time with faces only. Accuracy diminished. When they showed the photos of the tennis players' bodies only, however, the responses were again accurate. We "talk" with our bodies, too.

How many Boomers and Traditionalists, or even Gen Xers, would take seriously the young woman (tanned and fit) advertising a professional webinar using a photo of herself in a green fringed mini dress with a halter top, arms behind her head, butt pushed out, pouty lipped—right next to her seminar titles: "How to securing multiple job offers" and "Is there a trick to winning over hiring managers?" And yes—the first title included the typo.

HOW WE SAY IT

To Millennials, those Boomers and Traditionalists can seem too fixated on language. To Traditionalists, Gen Xers' word choices can seem imprecise, lack diplomacy, or be too pointed. Lay on top of those the issues of grammar, slang, and vocabulary and the chances of generational friction multiply.

Poor grammar and disorganization. Those with Twitter accounts have learned what 140 characters can contain—sometimes to the detriment of complete sentences. As thumbs punch out texts on touch screens, commas can be hard to come by.

Quite a few articles have quoted researchers hashing out concerns that these short bursts of communication, acronyms, and unpunctuated language will create a generation unable to put together a full sentence in Standard English. Traditionalists have worried that the *form* of communication reflects the loss of the writer's ability to think coherently, with order and precision. For them, writing begins with outlining and is evidence of clear thinking, with one explanation leading to the next thought in a march of progression.

More than one Traditionalist teacher has commented that the inability to write legibly is more than just a messy signature. For them, it indicates a lack of respect for the content and the reader. Whether it is true that scrawled letters equate to chaotic thinking, other generations should recognize that standard grammar, in speech and writing, in orderly paragraphs might mean more than you realize to older colleagues. To them, it communicates respect for yourself, your message, and the person receiving your message.

Slang

Different generations' communications styles and language evolved, obviously, at different points in history. References change:

- He was all decked out like Astor's pet horse.
- She was dressed to the nines.
- He looked like a million bucks.
- She was dressed to kill.

Each means essentially the same thing, but which one comes out of your mouth dates you. Where you grew up is an influence on idioms, as well. These expressions may cause a few puzzled glances—or more direct comments from Gen Xers who won't hesitate to speak up about quirky phrasing.

Beyond more common slang for which people can gather meaning from context and just pass by, generations' comfort levels with some language are different. Traditionalists and many Boomers find the phrases "that sucks" and "more bang for the buck" crude in a way that few younger people fathom.

Like the teacher who was "stoked," language choices leave an impression. Idioms matter to the audience. Among educators, particularly, Traditionalists may put an even higher premium on more formal Standard English.

Weak Versus Strong Language

Language motivates and creates disincentives. Use a generational lens to consider what persuades your listener. The chart offers suggestions on language that helps and hinders communication with different generations.

Language and Communication

Traditionalists	
Persuasive Language	**Turnoffs**
Authority	Profanity
Discipline	Slang
Dependable	Emotional language
Great	Disorganization
Respect	Lack of respect for tradition
Sacrifice	Poor grammar
Consistent	Disrespect for experience
Boomers	
Persuasive Language	**Turnoffs**
Consensus	Brusqueness
Human rights	Unfriendliness
Involvement	Not showing interest in the person
Relationship/Trust	Shows of power and one-upmanship
Team	Political incorrectness
Tolerance	Sports and war metaphors
Equal/Fair	Autocratic or threatening
	Opinionated
	Critical or blaming
	Exaggerated

Gen Xers	
Persuasive Language	**Turnoffs**
Alternatives	Schmoozing
Independent	Inefficient use of time
Efficient	Flashiness
Pragmatic	Exaggeration
Results-oriented	Bureaucracy, complex policies
Competence	Weak, tentative
	Apologetic or self-discounting
	Vague, ambivalent
Millennials	
Persuasive Language	**Turnoffs**
Achieve	Cynicism
Challenge	Sarcasm
Collaborate	Perceived unfairness
Community	Perceived condescension
Discovery	Autocratic or threatening
Future	Opinionated
Positive/fun	Critical or blaming
	Exaggerated

Source: Adapted from Raines (2003a) and Brandon and Seldman (2004).

Three tips can improve language across different generations:

- Be clear about whether you mean recommend or suggest—or whether you really mean expect. Boomers can read between the lines and may expect others to, but Millennials need things spelled out.
- Build on others' points of view by using "and" rather than "but." Try, "Yes, and . . . " rather than "but" or "however." Make your addition a mental adjustment—not just in the words you choose. The respect of affirming the other person's point of view goes a long way for any generation.
- Try alternative words that might soften without weakening the message: instead of *problem*, try *challenge*, *issue*, or *factor to consider.* Of course, if the matter is a more serious concern, by all means, say so. Boomers might be challenged by being more direct, Millennials and Xers by being more subtle.

WHERE AND *WHEN* WE SAY IT

The content of the message can be affected by the means used to communicate it and the timing. The generational lens is helpful in these cases, also.

Medium

The medium is the message, said Marshall McLuhan, the Canadian philosopher of communication theory. In other words, the form you use to convey your message also affects how it is perceived.

A Pew Internet & American Life Project survey finds that 63% of young people favor texting as their means of communication (Lenhart, 2009), followed by mobile phoning, messaging on social networking sites, and then instant messaging. As one teenager said, "If I called, I'd have to talk. And we might not have much to say. I'd have to go through all those things like, 'How are you?' Awkward!"

Boomers, conversely, may not be as tethered to their phones—or know where to find the text message function. Gen Xers may prefer e-mail, where the message is brief but more than the maximum number of characters allowed by most texts, and allows the receiver the flexibility of receiving and responding at a time best for that person.

Consider the chart in Figure 4.1, from 2007. Since then, although these data may not reflect it, texting seems to have become the medium of choice for most Millennials.

Figure 4.1 Means of Communication

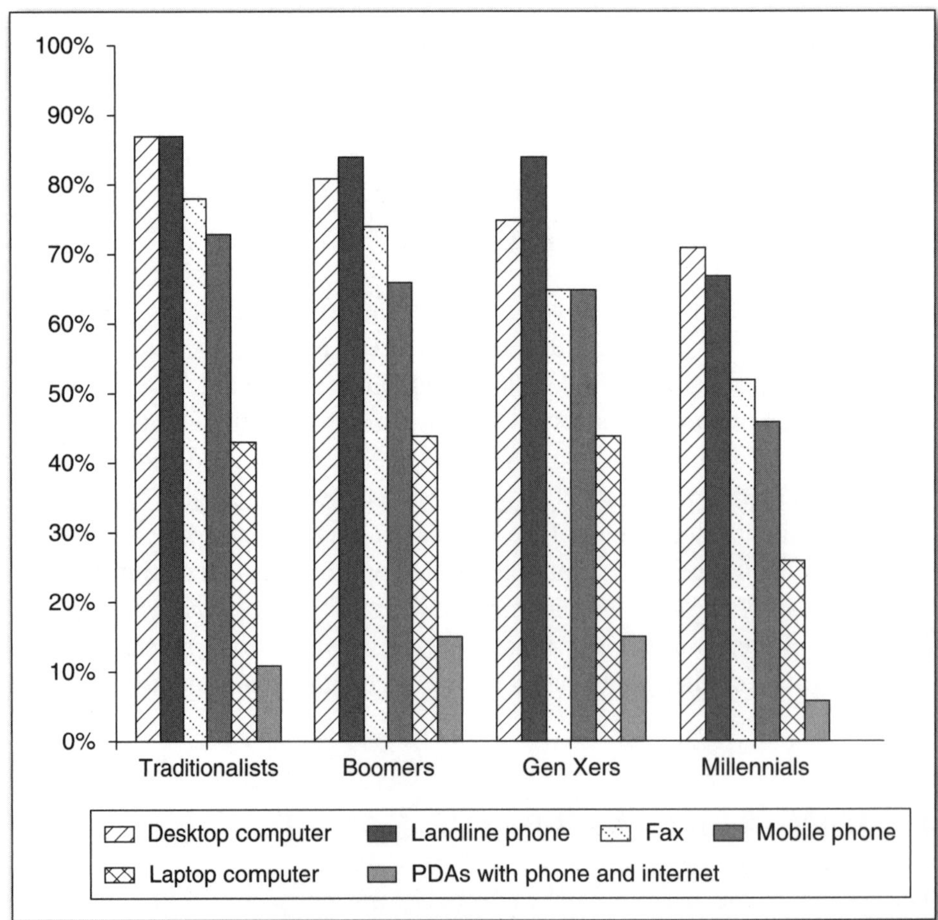

Source: Adapted from Randstad Work Solutions (2007).

A Randstad Work Solutions report (2012) found six out of 10 workers prefer face-to-face contact to phone or e-mail communication. Most people prefer personal communication, particularly when the content is sensitive.

The report found half of employees want normal, standard communication about things going on in the organization to come through e-mail. Newsletters, bulletin board, and phone calls barely made the list of preferred means of communication.

Conversely, critical communication about change should be taken care of in person, in a meeting with the affected group. The possibility of misinterpretation, generational or otherwise, is lessened when those affected have the opportunity to ask questions.

Time

One person's networking is another's ineffective use of time. What a Boomer sees as brusque or unfriendly is an Xer's view of efficiency, pragmatism, and results. One person sees "checking in" as a show of community, interest in the individual, while another generation might interpret the same action as a waste of time.

Keeping Boomers feeling connected and Xers feeling that not too much time was spent before getting down to business is a challenge. Remember that Boomers need more communication and Xers want to get their tasks done so they can get back to their lives.

Questions for Reflection

- What are the communication preferences for the generation of the person you're addressing?
- Are you communicating at the appropriate time?
- Are you using the appropriate medium for your communication with the other person (i.e., face-to-face, text, e-mail, memo)?
- Are you considering what you are communicating with your nonverbal language? (i.e., appropriate personal space, decorum for the situation)
- What group norms might you need to consider in framing your message? For example, does the group skew toward Boomers who want decisions based on deeper group discussion?
- Is the message appropriate? What is your purpose or desired outcome for your message? (What do you want the other person to know or understand?)
- What are your assumptions and values behind the communication?
- Are you listening to what others are saying—and what they intend? (listening for understanding)
- What does your voice sound like to others? Consider the volume, tightness of your vocal chords, shape of your mouth. Are you enunciating?
- Is your communication—voice and body language—matched to at least two other members of your team? If you are not matching the team "norm" for

(Continued)

(Continued)

communication, how can you bring yourself closer to the group's communication style?
- Do you have an open mindset—are you willing to receive what others have to say?
- Are you willing to work to understand the others' perspectives?
- Will you presume positive intent—that the person speaking is not speaking from a place of ill will?
- Are you waiting your turn to speak?
- Are you contributing to the conversation?
- Are you building on the other person's point of view? (using *and*, not *but*)
- Is your humor appropriate in others' eyes?

COLLABORATION

Patterns of communication are essential to successful teams. In fact, they are as important as individual intelligence, personality, skill, and the substance of the discussion combined, according to one Stanford study (Pentland, 2012). A team's energy and engagement with one another outside of meetings—from tone of voice, body language, whom they talked to, where and how much—was a predictor of how successful the team would be.

Every day in schools, learning teams of all sorts come together to plan lessons, assess student work, acquire new instructional strategies, and learn how to meet the needs of all learners. Yet teachers often aren't trained in effective group work. To improve team communications, consider five significant strategies.

1. **For Boomers, think "we."** Boomers are team players. The word "we" is important, and the idea of working together toward a goal has meaning. Boomers appreciate acknowledgments, accolades, and thank-yous for contributing to a bigger picture. The same feedback tactics are also important for Millennials.

2. **Think "loose-tight" with parameters for Xers.** Autonomy is the word. Xers appreciate independence and often feel that some agenda items could be handled better as e-mail, explanations could be shorter, or discussions more productive and effective with clearer expectations. Being mindful of time frames is important to keep Xers content.

3. **Millennials want to feel they have equality and status in the group.** Millennials began cooperative learning in preschool. The unspoken hierarchies or power structures that might diminish the voice of a new teacher would be frustrating to any new teacher, and especially a Millennial who believes in collaboration and co-creation, no matter the number of years of experience. Making sure that the opportunities for participation for Millennials are satisfying to them is key. Do they feel acknowledged? As said previously, Millennials want opportunities sooner and faster just like on Facebook, a flat platform for all voices to be heard equally, and they will expect the same in professional learning

communities. This can be a challenge for those Traditionalists or Boomers or Xers who have "been around the block" and expect their voices to hold greater sway over the group. Eyebrows have gone up in groups when Millennials suggest that the way things were done last year might not be working for them and a new way of doing the research paper or the annual "project" (pick the subject) sounds more up their alley. Millennials want to be a part of the team and want to express their voice to show engagement. It isn't a show of insubordination by a Millennial but a sign of commitment.

4. **Norm the group's language.** Xers want to know the rationale for what is being asked of them. Their questioning, "Why do we have to do it this way?" can rub others the wrong way and be perceived as attitude. The same is true with Millennials' asking, "Why can't we do it this way?" Learning to ask questions in a way that all generations can hear without defensiveness can begin with a facilitator who can help reframe the question or with group reminders: "Can you explain the rationale for how we are going about . . . " or "Can you help me understand the thinking behind. . . . " The right tone can keep a group on track.

5. **Respect all.** Jennifer Deal (2007) found perceptions around respect were a major source of generational conflict. In her research, she found that respondents felt that other generations were not behaving respectfully toward them. Deal found (p. 33) that what people meant by respect fell into three categories:

- Listen to me and pay attention to what I'm saying.
- Give my opinions the weight I believe they deserve.
- Do what I tell you.

Older generations want their opinions to carry more weight and for others to do what they said. Younger generations wanted others to pay attention and listen to them. Deal relates the story of a business in which an employee complained that a colleague was disrespectful toward the company leadership. With probing, the matter boiled down to the fact that this person showed the same manners/attitude/respect toward the receptionist that he showed the company president. The person was rude to neither, but his manner didn't change in the presence of authority, and where one person saw equality, another saw lack of respect.

Collaboration Across the Generations

Based on our own generational characteristics, we might want a colleague who . . .	
Traditionalists	• Is clear and concise • Is nonconfrontational • Communicates respect for the knowledge gained through experience • Thinks in terms of a greater goal • Acknowledges the hierarchy • Doesn't openly disagree • Uses correct grammar

(Continued)

(Continued)

Boomers	• Can speak about the profession in terms of values • Takes time in conversation to make a personal connection • Acknowledges experience • Isn't necessarily direct or blunt because Boomers read between the lines • Understands Boomers' need for protocols and policies • Avoids standing out from the group
Gen Xers	• Isn't afraid to answer "Why?" • Doesn't take bluntness personally • Can be clear and discuss consequences honestly • Is comfortable with transparency • Is OK with getting down to business without a lot of pleasantries • Doesn't judge when someone does the work just to get it done and move on to other things
Millennials	• Is able to use social networking communication (texting, tweeting, etc.) • Offers just-in-time support and access to materials • Listens without condescension • Offers frequent feedback • Doesn't always need to follow the process • Positive and motivational

A Communication Agreement

Teams could use this sample credo, or set of agreements, as a basis for intergenerational communications.

Our Team's Communication Credo

- We believe in mutual respect, open communication, and the willingness to listen to each other.
- We support the principle that we can respectfully agree to disagree and still meet our goals.
- We are willing to take responsibility for the quality and depth of our communication.
- We have a healthy intolerance for gossip, backbiting, and negativity.
- We do not assume to know the intentions behind each other's words or actions until we ask.
- We avoid using blame to deflect our responsibility for direct communication.
- When we have a disagreement with another team member, we will clear the air with that person.
- When we communicate together we will focus on
    - *Issues, situations, and tasks, not on persons*
    - *Observable behaviors and events*
    - *The here and now*
    - *Specifics rather than generalities*

- If we cannot resolve a conflict ourselves, we will schedule time to meet with our manager or another appropriate third party to help us work through our issues.
- We are willing to forgive one another when our imperfect communication results in misunderstandings and/or hurt feelings.
- We will hold one another accountable for the above principles and guidelines.

Source: Martin and Tulgan (2006, p. 132).

COMMUNICATION IS IMPORTANT

The generation gap, according to Deal (2007, p. 1) is "in large part the result of miscommunication and misunderstanding, fueled by common insecurities and the desire for clout—which includes control, power, authority, and position."

From greeting someone at the staff mailboxes in the main office while on the way to our classrooms to our daily lunch routines to our afterschool collaboration and staff meetings, day-to-day adult-to-adult communications in schools are moments when we build trust and make connections.

One Millennial found out the hard way about generational differences in communication. A Boomer boss worked closely in a small office with just a handful of others, all of whom were younger than she was. Although her office was the last door on the hallway, she kept her door open and encouraged the staff to greet her when they arrived in the morning and let her know as they left for the day (she kept typical Boomer work hours). The unspoken norm became an issue with one Millennial who did not catch on that everyone in the office was essentially "punching the clock" with the department head. The young woman went right to her desk in the morning without turning left to poke her head in on her boss. To the young woman, it was out of the way and out of her mind to travel down the hall to say good morning. At the end of the day, she was focused on getting home.

The Boomer, irritated, told the young woman, "My door is always open. Stop by." She made a joke about it a time or two. The Millennial missed the subtle directive. In a few months when her probation period ended, she found herself out of a job.

Tony Bryk and Barbara Schneider study the role of social relationships in schools and conclude that a base of trust in school heightens functioning and lets staff work at a higher level, achieving more ambitious goals (Gordon, 2002). They say that schools with higher levels of relational trust help raise student achievement because staff members are more able to make the kinds of changes that help students.

Relational trust is built through a variety of interactions and communications—following through on a request, keeping a promise, supporting ideas at a staff meeting, or using positive presuppositions in communications. There are many ways to make or break trust.

Deal (2007) found that people trust those they work with directly more than they trust "the system," and they trust upper management even less than they trust the system itself. This hierarchy of trust didn't vary by generation. Trust is an essential element of an effective workplace—and we trust people, not organizations. Lack of trust also leads to people leaving the organization. Retention becomes an issue, and recruitment challenges can follow, as we will see in the next chapter.

ACTIVITY 1

Four Corners

Objective: To generate an open discussion of ways to work more productively with other generations.

Time: 45 minutes.

Materials: Chart paper, markers.

Directions:

1. On chart paper, in advance of the meeting, post a set of guiding questions in each of the four corners of the room with a simple line scale drawn below each question.
2. Identify one corner of the room for each generation: Traditionalists, Boomers, Gen Xers, and Millennials.
3. Have the group members self-identify their own generation and gather in that corner.
4. Ask each group to decide to what extent that generation wants
   - to just get the work done,
   - to work collaboratively and ensure that everyone has input,
   - to consider the big picture before filling in details,
   - historical information/background before making a decision,
   - to consider everyone's feelings,
   - to avoid conflict at all costs,
   - to do whatever it takes—don't do it if you can't do it right, and
   - the who, what, when, how, and why details before taking action.
5. Have groups draw a visual scale representing the group's position on each point.
6. Ask individuals to choose a generation that they feel is most challenging to them to work with and to move to that corner.
7. Have the new group members discuss how the responses represented on the chart differ from their own generation's responses.
8. Each group should use the guiding question to frame the discussion. How might you as an individual work more productively with this generation?

ACTIVITY 2

Language Across the Generations

Objective: To understand language through a generational lens in order to be able to use language more effectively.

Time: Up to an hour depending on group size.

Materials: A copy of the table in this chapter, "Language and Communication," for each participant, a copy of the table with each generation on a separate piece of chart paper, markers.

Directions:

1. Work in pairs to generate an example for each box. Some examples are shown to get you started.
2. Share examples with the small group.
3. Ask representatives from each group to write examples for each category on the chart paper.
4. As a large group, discuss responses.
   - Do members of the generations feel the examples accurately represent persuasive language and turnoffs for their generation?
   - Do you have a story of when such an example was used and your reaction to it?
   - With your understanding of generational responses, would your reaction be the same today?
   - How might another generation respond to the same language?
   - What concepts would you add or subtract?

Table: Language and Communication

TRADITIONALISTS			
Persuasive language	**Examples**	**Turnoffs**	**Examples**
Authority	The superintendent has said that . . .	Profanity	
Discipline		Slang	
Dependable		Emotional language	
Great		Disorganization	
Respect		Lack of respect for tradition	
Sacrifice		Poor grammar	
Consistent		Disrespect for experience	
BOOMERS			
Persuasive language	**Examples**	**Turnoffs**	**Examples**
Consensus		Brusqueness	
Human rights		Unfriendliness	
Involvement		Not showing interest in the person	
Relationship/ Trust		Shows of power and one-upmanship	I've decided . . . I expect your cooperation . . . As head honcho . . .
Team		Political incorrectness	
Tolerance		Sports and war metaphors	
Equal/Fair		Autocratic or threatening	This is how it's going to go . . .
		Opinionated	Obviously, the right way is . . .
		Critical or blaming	You're being shortsighted. If you'd paid attention, you would have known . . .
		Exaggerated	This is the *only* way . . . *Anyone* can see that we need to . . .
GEN XERS			
Persuasive language	**Examples**	**Turnoffs**	**Examples**
Alternatives		Schmoozing	

(Continued)

(Continued)

Persuasive language	Examples	Turnoffs	Examples
Independent		Inefficient use of time	
Efficient		Flashiness	
Pragmatic		Hyperbole	
Results-oriented		Bureaucracy, complex policies	
Competence		Weak, tentative	Kind of . . . I think maybe . . . If it's OK with you . . .
		Apologetic or self-discounting	I hate to bother you, but . . . I'm sorry I haven't really thought this through . . . My team didn't have time . . . I'm not the best person at this job, but . . . You probably won't agree with me, but . . . I might be wrong . . .
		Vague, ambivalent	
MILLENNIALS			
Persuasive language	**Examples**	**Turnoffs**	**Examples**
Achieve		Cynicism	
Challenge		Sarcasm	I can't wait to hear what you've come up with now.
Collaborate		Perceived unfairness	
Community		Perceived condescension	The facts plainly show . . . Trust me on this; I ought to know.
Discovery		Autocratic or threatening	If you don't do this, I can find someone else who wants the job. I am not asking you; I am telling you.
Future		Opinionated	I know what I am talking about.
Positive/fun		Critical or blaming	This is a waste of my time. Suck it up.
		Exaggerated	It'll be a *total* disaster. It's *always* best to . . .

Source: Adapted from Raines (2003a) and Brandon and Seldman (2004).

ACTIVITY 3

Collaboration Questionnaire

Objective: To get to know your coworkers' generational styles and to inform each other of expectations and assumptions. These questions may be adapted for a mentor-mentee, coaching, supervisory, or team relationship.

Time: Varies depending on participants.

Materials: A copy of the questions for each.

Directions:

1. Schedule a conversation with your colleague(s).
2. In advance of the conversation, answer these questions:

   WORK STYLE

   - Describe your work style. Are you a "get things done right away" or a "give me a day or two to think about it" kind of worker?
   - Which tasks do you enjoy doing with others? Which tasks do feel better doing on your own?
   - What are your strengths as a worker? What about as a coworker? What do you feel are your learning edges?
   - What motivates you at work?
   - What situations/challenges/work assignments do you find fun? Which ones challenge you?
   - How do you handle interruptions or a change of plans? How might someone work best with you in those types of situations?

   COMMUNICATION STYLE

   - What are the best ways to communicate with you? Text, e-mail, in person, phone?
   - What is one thing about how you communicate that you would like to improve?
   - Do you tend to write in brief or be detailed? What types of direction do you need when you do an assignment—a bulleted list of to-dos with deadlines or just the gist of what is to be done?
   - How will others know you are hurt or upset? If you are upset, how do you want to be treated?
   - How do you like to handle mistakes? Yours or others?

   TEAMING

   - In a group situation, what are your strengths? What can you be counted on for? Keeping others on track, always bringing in another perspective?
   - What types of acknowledgments do you like? Public or private praise, tangible gifts, and so on.
   - In what situations do you ask for help? How do you feel about asking for help?
   - How would you like to receive feedback? In what forms?
   - What does the ideal team member look like to you?
   - What are your pet peeves in terms of team work/working with others/collaborating?

PERSONAL LIFE/PROFESSIONAL LIFE

- How much of your personal life do you like to share with those at work?
- Are you someone who socializes with colleagues from work? Lunch with those while at work?

3. Exchange responses for the other to read ahead of the conversation.
4. Spend time discussing the responses.
    - Which questions did you feel were the most important for the other person(s) to know?
    - Which questions did you find most difficult to answer?
    - How might your generational lens inform your response?
    - How might your generational lens affect your reaction to your colleagues' answers?

Source: Adapted from Ravinale (n.d.).

5 Recruiting and Retaining the Generations

According to Susan Moore Johnson, a professor of education at Harvard University's Graduate School of Education and director of the Project on the Next Generation of Teachers, the country's last large-scale hiring in education was 30 to 35 years ago. It was a time, she noted (2012), when women had fewer career options and teaching was an attractive option.

Today, the majority of those in postsecondary education are female, but women have many more career options. In addition, fewer men are in the workforce as a whole. Education is competing for new workers who have more choices than ever before.

And the need is growing. Draw a graph of teachers' years of experience with 0 to 26 along the X-axis and the result looks less like a bell curve and more like a wide U, according to Moore Johnson. Teachers with a year or two of experience and teachers who are completing their education careers dominate the graph.

Those with less experience also may not remain in education. Although Boomers went into teaching for a lifelong career, the generations following them have a series of jobs or careers, with some researchers showing that these workers are having between four and seven different jobs or more. Moore Johnson said just 17 of 50 young teachers interviewed expected to remain in education for their entire career.

Other statistics show that the number of teaching positions, at least before the Great Recession, had increased over several decades, likely driven up by class size limits and more students with special needs attending school after the 1970s.

The future teaching corps, then, will look very different. According to Ingersoll and Merrill (n.d.), "(T)eaching will be practiced predominantly by beginners and the young. But beginners, the largest group of the largest occupation, are also the least stable and, our analysis also shows, that instability has been increasing" (Conclusion section, para. 3).

Districts will be challenged to create a model of recruitment that will continually fill the openings. The flip side, though, is an incentive for districts to work to retain educators who are already in the system. "Unless we are more supportive, we're going to have rapid turnover," Moore Johnson said.

Using a generational lens to view generations' different needs and expectations can help districts in their efforts to recruit and retain employees. If you're working in a group, you could begin your work with this chapter with Activity 2. It might provide an engaging start to working with the information to follow.

RECRUITING

As recently as 1999–2000, six in 10 educators were Boomers, according to the Schools and Staffing survey, with about 16 years of teaching experience.

By the end of this decade, the Bureau of Labor Statistics (Toossi, 2002) projects a vastly different workforce. Of every 10 employees:

- Two will be Boomers
- Two will be Gen Xers
- Four to five will be Millennials
- One to two will be the new generation, post-Millennials

Recruiting, retaining, and managing the generations are intertwined elements of the same issue. Let's start with deepening our understanding about the new 20-somethings, who will be the majority of recruits.

A New Timetable for Adulthood

- One-third of 20-somethings change addresses in a year.
- Four of 10 people in their 20s move in with their parents at least once.
- The median age for women to marry was 26 in 2009, and 28 for men, five years later than in the 1970s.

Source: Marantz Henig (2010).

Beginning Teachers May Be Emerging Adults

Sociologists suggest that the transition to adulthood is marked by completing school, moving out of your parents' home, supporting yourself financially, getting married, and becoming a parent yourself. In 1960, three out of four women and 65% of men had done *all five* of these things by the age of 30. A lot of Traditionalists and Boomers will have a mindset that 20-somethings today are a lot like 20-somethings from the past.

In 2000, fewer than half of 30-year-old women and one-third of men had accomplished these markers of adulthood.

Frank Furstenberg of the MacArthur Foundation Research Network on Transitions to Adulthood called the idea that people enter adulthood in their late teens or early 20s "archaic."

"Where once youth moved nearly lockstep through the markers of adulthood," the Network found, "today . . . that path is much more circuitous and steeped in ambiguity. Jobs are no longer secure, marriage is delayed, buying a house and gaining an education are expensive, relationships are more tenuous, and the connection to community more fractured."

We're in a time of great social change. More people are cohabiting rather than marrying, the median age for marriage is five years later than it was just a few decades ago, and other reports have found that more young people now view getting married and having children as "lifestyle choices" (Cohen, 2010).

It's no wonder that young people are confused about their entry into the adult world. Consider this: 18-year-olds can vote for president and join the military, but can't drink until they're 21. Some states allow 14-year-olds to begin driver training, but car rental companies require drivers to be 25. National health care policy now will consider those under 26 dependents, but parents can't look at their children's college records if the child is 18 (Marantz Henig, 2010).

The result is showing up in movies and article after article in the media. The blame frequently is put on "helicopter parents," but the truth is that culturally, we have slowed the pace at which young people become the old definition of "adult."

More than one human resources professional has told the tale of the prospective employee who shows up at the interview with his or her mother. Or of answering the phone to find a parent on the line asking questions about benefits or other job details for the new employee.

In another case, a new teacher had been on the job and seemed to be adjusting well, fitting into the grade-level team, managing logistics within the elementary school building, and handling her class seemingly without too much trouble. Then the principal's secretary got a call "reporting an absence." The teacher was going to be out of school on Thursday, the teacher's mother told the surprised secretary, "for a mandatory family engagement." The teacher had not notified the office, just the mother.

We can shake our heads about these stories—or we can recognize the new reality and the need to mentor new staff as we work through the process of recruiting and ensure greater efforts to train and retain them.

Recruiting Through a Generational Lens

Schools aren't the only ones facing challenges in hiring.

"Current hiring practices are haphazard at best and ineffective at worst," note Fernandez-Araoz, Groysberg, and Nohria (2009) in the *Harvard Business Review.* "And even when companies find the right people, they have difficulty retaining them." The authors provide a common sense outline of recruiting steps.

Anticipate the Needs

Businesses that have exemplary practices, such as Southwest Airlines, McKinsey, Intuit, TCS, or ServiceMaster, invest in proactive plans to fill staffing needs, according to Fernandez-Araoz, Groysberg, and Nohria (2009).

That begins with regularly analyzing future needs and evaluating the pool of potential talent, rather than waiting until openings occur.

Does your district or school review staffing every two to three years and answer the following questions:

- How many people will we need in the next three years? In what positions?
- What qualities do we want in the people in those positions? How will we recognize those qualities?
- What might the organizational structure look like?
- What do we need in our pipeline today to ensure we can meet our future needs?

Older generations may not have made it a habit to project forward potential needs.

Specify the Job

Some school districts have not updated their job descriptions in decades. The district likely has been reorganized in that time and had changes in strategy or focus. Job descriptions need to align with those changes and outline current responsibilities.

A job description defines the position's specific requirements, skills needed, and experience desired. It also might be useful to describe what other positions interact with this one. A comprehensive job description should include the following:

- Job title and summary of responsibilities
- Essential tasks that the job requires
- Minimum qualifications, including licenses and certificates
- Description of working conditions
- Information about supervisors, managers, and others with whom the position interacts
- Desired qualifications, such as experience and specialized knowledge
- An equal opportunity employment statement
- The "other duties as assigned" caveat

The U.S. Department of Labor, Employment & Training Administration created the Occupational Information Network, O*NET (www.onetonline.org/), which offers a good list of tasks for specific positions and can be a starting place for building job descriptions.

Job descriptions increasingly should be essential, not only for recruiting and hiring, but as an element of employee evaluations. The job description, through evaluation, also can be linked to professional development.

Millennials, especially, find it helpful to see as many particulars as possible for potential positions.

Develop the Applicant Pool

This is an area where creativity can reign. The pool may not be very deep for filling future positions. Districts may need to sell themselves to attractive candidates. Although some have experience doing so when looking for math, science, or special education teachers, or may have developed some strategies for hiring candidates of color, those strategies may need to be expanded and broadened to include other positions.

Where can you recruit? Some districts begin with high school clubs of future teachers, look to local universities, seek out states that export high numbers of new teacher graduates, look for layoffs, and participate in on-site or Internet job fairs.

Posting positions on the district website just may not be enough. Millennials used to using RSS feeds and social media to get information pushed into their inboxes may not be prepared to seek out individual website postings. Sell the position. Can you link directly to a potential coworker's reference? Can you show instead of telling, using videos? Link to the principal's blog? The superintendent's Twitter feed? Use social media?

The Internet generation, used to communicating all the time, anywhere, is a potential resource. Peer recommendations are, as ever, a good source of candidates—ask peers for names but also let their social media networks know of specific openings.

Savvy human resources departments cast a wide net in today's social media universe. Online may be the biggest job fair yet (see illustration 5.1).

Illustration 5.1 Screen Capture of an Online Job Fair Advertisement

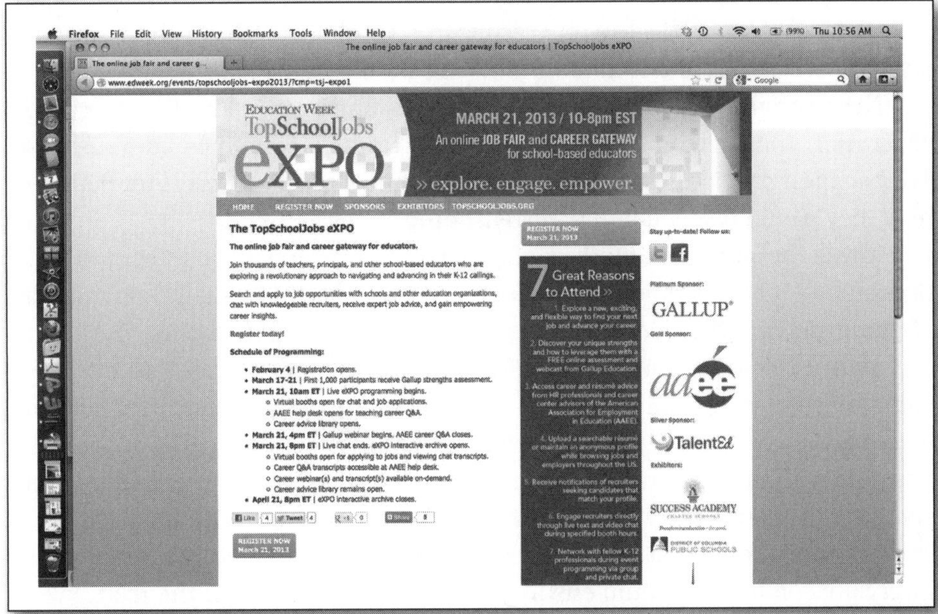

More districts are thinking, too, about nontraditional candidates. Could that Latin teaching position be taken over part time by a retiree? Would that volunteer parent make a good paraprofessional or parent liaison? Which "outsiders" who interact with the school might, with a little extra credentialing, be able to fill a needed spot? Are there consultants who might fit the bill, either as employees or as long-term contractors?

Moore Johnson notes that four of every 10 new teachers today are coming from another field with work experience outside of education. She said the average age for an alternative entrant to the teaching profession is 35.

How deep should the final pool be? Fernandez-Araoz, Groysberg, and Nohria (2009) say the ideal is 10 to 12 carefully generated candidates.

A principal had just interviewed a student teacher and decided he was not going to give her the job. He struggled with how to give her feedback. He was perplexed as to why the student's master teacher hadn't helped her realize that she should have had a formal lesson plan for her model lesson and that she shouldn't have worn flip-flops. He struggled with how to help her understand the impression she had left. Did he really have to tell her that there is an implicit dress code during model lessons? Did he really have to specify that she turn in a written plan?

Hire

The ideal interview group not only is motivated, but also has training. Some research has shown that even hiring at random may be better than hiring a person recommended by poor interviewers. Some young Millennials now are in supervisory positions and may never have interviewed candidates before. Interviewing is a skill set that should be learned—and taught. Fernandez-Araoz, Groysberg, and Nohria (2009) say that relying on "gut feel" that a candidate has what it takes is too subjective and results in poor choices. The authors say such personal preference and traditions in hiring should be avoided.

They recommend that the interview committee include the position's supervisor, that person's supervisor, and a human resources administrator. They suggest providing simulated situations and asking prospects for details of how they would respond and their reasoning.

"Given the ad hoc quality, lack of specified criteria and inconsistency of practices among the companies we studied, it's no wonder that usually about a third of promising new hires depart within three years of being recruited," they write.

Another element that may be adding to earlier departures is that interview committees may not interview on site. Candidates have been hired without meeting the colleagues they'll be teaching with, sometimes without spending any time with their potential department chair or learning team leader. Making sure that the candidate will fit in with the team is essential with the need today to work more collaboratively. Although the logistics may be challenging, the interview committee should ensure that final candidates and the team take a little time to interact before a final decision is made.

One small suburban district was faced with several elementary schools needing a new principal in the following year. There was a lot of handwringing since the district had only two middle schools with one assistant principal each. One teacher leader the district administrators had cultivated was thinking more about retirement than a promotion, and another had recently left the district for a job elsewhere because he was discouraged. District leaders had a pool of candidates from the surrounding area but narrowed the list to in-district candidates only, saying they were afraid "outsiders won't 'get' our culture." They ended up with just a handful of candidates and, in the end, at least one unpopular and ineffective principal.

RETAINING

The National Commission on Teaching and America's Future (Carroll, 2007) reports that teacher turnover could be costing the country as much as $7 billion a year. Moore Johnson (2012) said the cost of turnover can be estimated by experience: $10,547 per first-year teacher, $18,617 to replace a second-year teacher, and $26,687 for a third-year teacher. Beyond dollars, she said, turnover affects student performance, especially with low-income students where a series of less experienced teachers in a row can have a dramatic negative effect on outcomes. Turnover in staff can also disrupt the school culture, keep effective teaching teams from forming, and keep principals more focused on replacing teachers than on building teams.

Retention once was less of an issue, according to Moore Johnson (2012), because the generation facing retirement now went into teaching expecting to remain in education for their whole career, or even to remain in the same school and the same classroom. Millennials, who are reviving that sense of civic-mindedness, increasingly plan to make teaching a lifelong career.

Millennials cite the three most important factors in choosing a career as: involving work they love (83%), allowing time to be with family (81%), and contributing to society and helping others (72%).

Despite their intentions, however, teachers under 30 left the profession at a rate 51% higher than older teachers, and turnover has been increasing for the last 20 years (Coggshall, Behrstock-Sherratt, & Drill, 2011). Although just 31% of Gen Xers expect to leave their employer in less than five years, 52% of Millennials do (Shaffer, 2008).

So what happens between idealism and daily classroom life? Moore Johnson notes that teachers who "know what they're getting into are more likely to stick with it" (2012). She said a survey of districts in four states of when teachers were hired showed 38% were hired more than a month before the start of school, 29% were hired a month before—and a full third were hired *after* the year started.

Orientation to help newcomers acclimate *before* the year begins might affect the outcome. One young teacher went to her principal just a few weeks into the school year. She was in tears. She'd studied pedagogy and knew the subject matter. "I just didn't think it was going to be so *hard,*" she confessed. Pushing back the joke that teaching is always easier when the students aren't there, the principal kindly asked her what was causing her the most difficulty. "I thought they would give me the lessons and I'd teach," she said. "This is hard work."

Instead of sending her off, the principal used the moment to reexamine "the way we do things around here." He asked probing questions about how she had learned key information about school routines. He asked how she was accessing mentoring and coaching opportunities and how she was interacting with grade-level peers. He helped her understand her job description and how to access support, and then he used their time to tap into her creativity. Finally, he charged her with talking to other first-year teachers in the building and a neighboring building whose principal he knew well to generate some ideas for making the transition smoother, stimulating her desire to take charge and demonstrating trust in her abilities that motivated her to keep going.

In your school or district, how often does a mentor check in with teachers who have fewer than five years of experience? Are coaches available? How often does the principal stop by the teacher's classroom? What does the principal do to develop a culture of support in the building? How are teams developed and supported? How is the orientation program evaluated?

Martin and Tulgan, authors of *Managing the Generation Mix: From Urgency to Opportunity* (2006), also suggest asking whether supervisors understand generational needs and are able to offer informed support; Millennials might need help understanding when to arrive and leave the building, time management skills, and other basics.

Four in 10 new teachers are entering education as a second career at an average age of 35, according to Moore Johnson (2012). These teachers will have different expectations, different needs, and different motivations.

Findings From Young Teachers

A Sense of Calling: Who Teaches and Why (Public Agenda, 2000) focused on new teachers entering the profession and observations of those hiring and supervising the young teachers. The study found the following:

- 96% of new teachers (in the classroom for five years or less) said they were teaching because they love the work, and eight in 10 would choose teaching again if starting over.
- Three-fourths view their profession as a "lifelong choice."
- Approximately half of administrators said the quality of new teachers had improved, with another 39% saying it had remained about the same.
- About seven in 10 new teachers cited the lack of potential for advancement as a deterrent for those considering the profession.
- Young people in the survey said the lack of respect for teachers and the threats to physical safety were downsides to an education career.
- 86% of new teachers said smaller class sizes would help improve teaching, followed by requiring secondary school teachers to major in the subject they teach and increasing professional development opportunities.
- Most favor higher salaries for those who work in challenging schools, but not higher pay for harder-to-staff subject teachers.
- In addition, the 2009 MetLife Survey of the American Teacher found that 62% of Millennial teachers agreed that "other teachers contribute to my success in the classroom," and nearly the same number of Gen Xers agreed. Less than half of Boomers did.

Earlier chapters describe characteristics of the generations. Districts and schools that want to retain the generations may consider how to adapt to meet the needs of different generations.

What might a retention plan look like if it were designed to address the needs outlined for two key generations?

Millennials:

- Want flexibility in work hours
- Need frequent, daily feedback
- Need praise
- Are sensitive to criticism
- Want to work in teams
- Expect to be part of things and that their "expertise" will be listened to
- Are open to sharing their practice and want to observe other teachers
- Are task-oriented
- Want time for their own interests
- Are more focused on their relationship with their supervisor than the school or district
- Want to *see* that they are making a difference
- Expect access to decision makers and quick promotions
- Want up-to-date technology and communications (consider that 83% of Millennials sleep with their cell phones next to their bed, according to a Pew Research Center survey [2010a & b], compared with just half of Boomers)
- Need clear and specific next steps
- Favor differentiated pay—perhaps through recognizing National Board Certification, top evaluations, student performance, or difficulty of assignment
- Are used to being rewarded just for showing up
- Have not yet developed ways to cope with stress and daily struggles

Bruce Tulgan, author of *Not Everyone Gets a Trophy* (2009), suggests giving Millennials a sense of context and working with them specifically to help them manage themselves. He said some Millennials find checklists and activity logs useful.

Tulgan related the example of a warehouse supervisor who assigned employees points for their work. The employees could use the points for bonuses, to leave early, or for time off—their choice. At first glance, this is a business-focused solution. However, might a principal be specific about steps to take toward team leadership roles? Specify the rewards for extra work—such as leaving a few minutes early one day or offering, if money is available, a token such as a coffee gift card?

Tulgan suggests that Millennials want to hear that they'll be recognized for performance and will get credit for their achievements. He suggests giving them a clear set of responsibilities; not being subtle, but being sensitive to Millennials' need for praise; finding areas they can control; and asking, What do you need from me? Followed by, OK, and here's what I need from you.

Gen Xers:

- Want to know, What's in it for me?
- Look for opportunities to develop new skills for career development
- Like flexible work arrangements
- Want coaches and mentors for the Xers' own talent development
- Desire access to decision makers
- Look for increasing responsibility
- Are seeking ways to feel compensated for their contributions

Some incentives and rewards for Gen Xers include training in marketable skills; more control over their schedules; some choice in coworkers; some say–so over their assignments.

Although recruiting Boomers may not be a priority and districts and schools may think of Boomers and Traditionalists as retiring rather than needing to be retained, shrinking numbers of 35- to 45-year-old potential midlevel managers in the labor pool should cause leaders to take another look.

Boomers and Traditionalists

The National Council on Teaching and America's Future (Foster, 2010) reports that many veteran teachers would stay on in education if they had new challenges or part-time opportunities.

In addition, NCTAF says second-career Boomers are good candidates for providing leadership expertise in new roles.

The report states that six of 10 Boomer teachers intend to work after retiring from their current jobs, and 70% are interested in working in new roles in education. According to the NCTAF video *Did You Know?* (www.learningteams.org), nearly four in 10 want to return part time.

The NCTAF suggests using Traditionalists and Boomers in new ways "to continue to strengthen the fabric of public education":

- Adjunct teachers working alongside classroom teachers to support students.
- Coaches or mentors to help teachers improve their craft.
- Content advisers to offer their subject expertise, help with lesson planning, or work directly with students.
- Project coordinators to work on short-term, class, or after-school assignments such as a science fair. In an NCTAF-NASA project in Maryland, retired teachers help new teachers develop project-based learning units that align with state curriculum and assessment standards.
- Tutors to provide direct student support in an area of need or for enrichment.
- Other roles, including community liaison, public relations consultant, grants manager/writer, after-school program coordinator and workshop leader. In another example in the report, a retired marketing executive helped the district administration plan and present a technology innovation to the school board. Its successful implementation led the district to become an educational technology leader in the state.

One caveat we'd like to add: Those who have been gone from the workplace for more than a few years can lose touch with how current policies and practices have affected classroom practice. Those in charge should make sure that more veteran coaches are up to speed with initiatives, pedagogy, technology, and protocols. District administrators need to monitor the relationship between the coach and coachee so that coaching takes place in the present rather than unhelpful conversations about "what it used to be like when I worked in this district," an uncomfortable situation for a coachee.

Susan Moore Johnson of Harvard's Graduate School of Education outlined three types of professional cultures (2012):

The veteran-oriented professional culture has a high proportion of experienced teachers and established patterns of practice, some of which are effective and some of which are not. The staff is friendly, but new teachers are not integrated into the work. Teachers stay busy in their own classrooms or leave after the last bell. They've done this work for decades and don't have to plan much.

The novice-oriented professional culture is a staff of mostly new teachers who are very intense about their work. There may be a few midcareer changers in the mix, but these are teachers with a cause. They may be working in high-needs schools to try to enact a turnaround. They generally are working with little professional guidance, Moore Johnson said.

Integrated professional cultures have an ongoing exchange between expert and novice teachers who take collective responsibility for the school and student and teacher learning. The veterans are "sparked" by the younger teachers' attitudes, and new teachers learn from the veterans.

These cultures matter a great deal. After a year, Moore Johnson said, she found:

	New teachers still teaching after one year	**Still teaching in the same school after one year**
Veteran-oriented culture	75%	57%
Novice-oriented culture	83%	67%
Integrated culture	88%	82%

"Schools could be staffed like summer camps, with turnover and no increase in professional capacity," Moore Johnson said (2012). "Or teachers could have a differentiated career that scaffolds their expertise with roles such as mentors, instructional coaches, data analysts, staff developers, cluster leaders, department heads, peer reviewers."

Across the Generations

Engaging employees is as important as engaging students. What motivates people, particularly educators, is obviously not their salaries. The work itself is the motivation. Purpose gets people up in the morning. And psychologists find that recognition and praise go a long way to keep most people motivated.

Robert Eckert, in *The Two Most Important Words* (2013), advises making time every week to acknowledge good work, hand-writing thank-you notes, and publicly praising people in a specific, timely way. Psychologists are finding that praise and recognition, in addition to building culture, can be more important motivators than money. *The Carrot Principle: How the Best Managers Use Recognition to Engage Their People, Retain Talent, and Accelerate Performance,* by Adrian Gostick and Chester Elton, is a good resource for understanding motivation.

Studies have found that in teams where people have not received any praise or recognition, the group's productivity, morale, and engagement tend to be lower. In addition, turnover is likely to be higher. In contrast, when businesses have higher morale and employee engagement, turnover is less likely and productivity is higher.

Studies also find that supervisors' perceptions of how often they praise and recognize staff may be different from employees' perceptions. A brief, anonymous poll could be revealing.

FOCUS ON RECRUITING AND RETAINING

Teacher turnover, what some term "churn," continues to be rampant and affects students directly. We need new strategies and ideas for addressing the current situation and the new needs of different generations. As more Traditionalists and Boomers retire, the brain drain will only increase.

Finding new and creative ways to address both recruitment and retention is imperative in order to best serve kids, yet another way schools will need to adapt.

Who You'll Be Hiring

Since 1998, Beloit College has released an annual Mindset List looking at cultural touchstones for entering freshmen. Today's students don't need phones in their dorm rooms—they probably don't remember landlines. They may first see their roommate's face on Facebook rather than in person. Human resources managers should take note. These people will be in the job market very, very soon.

For the freshman college class of 2013:

- The Green Giant has always been Shrek, not the big guy picking vegetables.
- They have never had to use a card catalog to find a book.
- Salsa has always outsold ketchup.
- Chocolate chip cookie dough ice cream has always been a flavor choice.
- They have never had to "shake down" an oral thermometer.
- They have never understood the meaning of RSVP.

- American students have always lived anxiously with high-stakes educational testing.
- Condoms have always been advertised on television.
- There has always been a Cartoon Network.
- The nation's key economic indicator has always been the Gross Domestic Product (GDP).
- Women have always outnumbered men in college.
- We have always watched wars, coups, and police arrests unfold on television in real time.
- There have always been flat-screen televisions.
- They have always eaten Berry Berry Kix.
- Everyone has always known what the evening news was before the evening news came on.
- Britney Spears has always been heard on classic rock stations.
- For one reason or another, California's future has always been in doubt.
- Two Koreas have always been members of the United Nations.
- There has always been blue Jell-O.

Source: College Mindset List by Tom McBride and Ron Nief.

ACTIVITY 1

Recruiting for the New Millennium

Objective: To view the school or district from the perspective of a potential job seeker from a technologically savvy generation.

Time: 10 minutes, plus time for discussion.

Materials: Access to the Web and a copy of this tool for each participant.

Directions:

1. Check your online presence. Using search engines, enter your school or district name. What are the first 10 entries under your school or district name? Does your official website come up in the top 10? If it does not, your online presence is suffering.
2. Try more than one search engine. The largest are Google and Bing.
3. On your website, find:
   - The address (including state) and phone number.
   - The name of a key contact person for your school or district.
   - A link to the site map.

   If these items are not on your home page, consider adding them.
4. Take the role of savvy computer job searcher. Write the number of click-throughs (pages) you went to in order to locate:
   - A "contact us" button to have questions answered.
   - The human resources page.
   - Information about benefits.
   - A job application.
   - A way to submit a resume online.
   - Details about the school or district, such as number of staff, students, highlights.
   - The school year calendar.

   How difficult was it to find these items?
5. Take the role of a new teacher in your school or district. Can you find:
   - A teacher contract?
   - A salary schedule?
   - An orientation packet?
   - District professional development opportunities?
   - Insurance information?
   - Benefits?
   - Policies and procedures?
6. Take a balcony view of your home page. What impression does it convey? What three adjectives come to mind when you view it? Compare your adjectives with those of colleagues from other generations.

ACTIVITY 2

Fact Check

Take this quiz, based on U.S. information, before reading the chapter to determine what you may already know. As a group, find the answers in the chapter and compare the correct information with your responses. Determine what next steps you might want to take based on your new information.

Mark true or false next to each item:

1. ______ Most teachers have five to 10 years of experience.
2. ______ Half of Millennials expect to leave their employer in less than five years.
3. ______ Half of Gen Xers expect to leave their employer in less than five years.
4. ______ The average age for a beginning teacher who has an alternative certification is 25.
5. ______ More Boomers than Millennials believe that "other teachers contribute to my success in the classroom."
6. ______ Four of every 10 new teachers today have work experience in another field.
7. ______ New teachers with fewer than five years of experience are overwhelmingly choosing the education profession because of the work hours.
8. ______ The majority of administrators believe the quality of new teachers is the same as or better than in the past.
9. ______ The major deterrents to those considering teaching is the lack of potential for advancement.
10. ______ New teachers' first choice for improving teaching conditions is smaller class sizes.
11. ______ Millennials favor paying teachers more for teaching hard-to-staff subjects, such as math and science, and for working in high-poverty schools.
12. ______ The greatest proportion of those leaving the profession is older teachers.
13. ______ In 2020, half the labor force is expected to be Millennials.
14. ______ The majority of teachers are hired more than a month before school starts.
15. ______ More than half of teachers intend to continue working after retiring from their present jobs.

Answers: 1. F; 2. T; 3. F; 4. F; 5. F; 6. T; 7. F; 8. T; 9. T; 10. T; 11. F; 12. F; 13. T; 14. F; 15. T.

ACTIVITY 3

Incentives and Rewards

Review what incentives and rewards are available to staff in your school or district. Next, be creative in considering what options might be available that could affect recruitment and retention.

With your group, discuss and note your answers to the following:

- Considering that seven in 10 new teachers cite the lack of potential for advancement as a deterrent for those considering the profession, what might the district *do* that would motivate potential educators? How would it communicate any decisions with potential teachers?
- Many prospective teachers are concerned about physical safety and a lack of respect for teachers. How might the district address these concerns?
- The majority of new teachers want smaller class sizes and professional development opportunities. What is available in your district or school? How do prospective teachers find this information?
- The majority of Millennial and Gen-X teachers surveyed agreed that "other teachers contribute to my success in the classroom." What does the school or district do that would attract the teachers who agreed with this statement?
- When have you been able to arrange your work in a way that motivated you to stay in your position?
- What nonmonetary rewards have made you feel valued in your career?
- How might the incentives you listed become part of the school or district culture? Who would need to be involved in making them a regular part of the workplace?

ACTIVITY 4

New Teacher Checklist

Those charged with professional development might consider which of these points need to be covered *before* or *during* the first week of school to help new teachers acclimate. Review which points are covered in your current orientation and which might be helpful to add in order to improve teacher retention.

Priorities Before the First Week

- If the teacher is in a secondary school and in a department, and the department has an office, do the new teachers know where they will sit? Any reason to position their desks in certain places? Near certain colleagues? Does someone need to move so the new teacher can be closer to mentors or the department chair? Does the department usually sit together at staff meetings? Who will bring the new teacher to the meeting?
- Are the new teachers seated near other colleagues during the orientation? Are they near colleagues who teach the same subject or the same students? Is it possible to have them be near someone who will be supporting them?
- Have supplies a new teacher might need for his/her room been ordered (paper clips, staplers, textbooks, curricular materials, etc.)?
- In looking around the room(s) the new teachers are in, what additional support should they have to help them teach and manage most effectively in that environment (information on arranging seating, lab conditions, etc.)?
- Are the new teachers sharing a room with another teacher? Is the colleague who is sharing the room clear about his or her expectations for a room arrangement? Will that colleague support the new teacher in getting space within the room?
- Does each new teacher have syllabi and course materials for each of the subjects/courses he or she will teach? Is the information accessible to them online or could it be given to them?
- Does the new teacher receive a laptop with necessary applications or a computer in his or her room? If the teacher does not have a laptop, who does the teacher need to talk to?
- Has the new teacher been given an e-mail address and access?
- Does the new teacher have access to student data and know how to interpret and use the data?
- Does the new teacher know how to upload to the school grade-book system?
- Is the new teacher trained on the school's preference for how to do a Web page and what should be on it?
- Is a new teacher orientation happening at the school building? If so, who is running it? Do you have a description of what will be covered at the site level so you can review and add department specifics that won't be covered?
- Does the site-level orientation address arrival and departure times, attendance, keys, parking?
- Does the new teacher understand professional protocol for daily work, such as what to send and not send through e-mail, the importance of taking class attendance daily and how to do so, and so on?
- Has the school orientation helped introduce new teachers to the school copy machine system, policies/timelines? Does the new teacher know how to make copies on the department/school machine? Does he or she have a code if one is needed?
- Do the mentor and the new teacher(s) have a prep period in common? If not, is there a plan or a regular time for how the two will communicate?

- What plans are in place to help new teachers with long-term planning and pacing? How long may they have certain books before returning them? Do they know the number of weeks/days they should be doing certain units? How will this information be communicated?
- How will walk-throughs and/or informal observations be conducted in the first few days, weeks, and half of the quarter before warning notices are due or before parent-teacher conferences?
- When will you explain your job and what the role entails? What should new teachers come to you for, and for what should they go to others in the administration?
- Are the veteran teachers aware of who will be new to the department/school and/or who will be new to the grade level or course?

To Be Covered During the First Few Weeks

- When will new teachers learn about the evaluation system and the district's system of informal and formal observations?
- How will the administration be introduced to the new teachers? How will they know whom to go to for what? What type of encounters should the new teacher have with administrators? Should the new teachers introduce themselves to the administration or wait until administrators come to meet them/observe them, etc.?
- If you have videos or resources that are department/grade-level related, do new teachers have and know how to use the system for accessing them?
- Does the school expect all staff to do adjunct duty? If so, how are the expectations explained to new staff? If new teachers are exempt from the duty, how might they participate in school and community in other ways so they are seen as being involved?
- Who will explain to the new teacher the policies on student tardies and cuts, which forms to send to parents, where the forms are, how to fill them out, levels of penalties, and so on? Whom does the new teacher notify if absences are excessive?
- What do new teachers need to do with the list of absences for sports/field trips? Do they mark students who are absent and not worry about it?
- Does the new teacher know the counselors, the speech language pathologist, the psychologist, and their roles? Does the new teacher understand when to get these colleagues involved and for which issues?
- Does the new teacher understand how he or she might have students moved in or out of classes? Can the teacher offer feedback to the counselor/principal?
- Does the secretary (if your department or school has one) have a job description the new teacher will need to know about so the teacher isn't asking for something inappropriate from the secretary or knows what assistance *is* offered?
- Is there a protocol for asking new teachers about their strengths, areas for improvement, and concerns to help begin to figure out how to work with those strategically more immediately?
- Does the school/department have a protocol for parent complaints/problems/conferences? Who handles the complaint first/second? Is there a timeline for getting back to a parent? When should a new teacher come to a supervisor with a parent concern? How will the supervisor explain when he or she will be the one to handle a complaint?
- Are there expectations about grading—what types of grades are offered, how they are weighted, rubrics, and so on? Is there a suggested timeline for returning student work? Is there a way to help the new teacher calibrate with others within the department/course/level?
- Do new teachers know who to ask for technological support? For hardware problems versus software requests?

- Are grade-level/course-specific teams set up?
- Is there a protocol for sharing and maintaining resources so colleagues return materials in a timely manner?
- Are new teachers working with veterans on the same grade level or in the same course? Have the veterans been informed? What are the expectations for the experienced teachers on the amount of time spent with a course-alike colleague?
- Within a grade or a team, does everyone know his or her role and responsibility? How will new teachers be introduced to the group, and how will they learn the norms and responsibilities? Does the leader need support in facilitation, coaching, or collaboration? Do veteran members need a review about what effective collaborative behavior looks like?
- Is it clear to all how to communicate with one another? Are there changes needed in e-mail etiquette? Putting items on one's desk?
- Are there or will there be changes in personnel midyear because of maternity leave, sick leave, or retirements that will change someone's status, job description, or percentage of work (for this year or even next year)?
- Has a teacher changed grade levels or courses? Moved to work with AP students or to work with lower level students? Moved into direct instruction? Moved from another school within the district or another grade? Will the teacher need additional support on content, student management, culture?
- Will there be changes in textbooks, materials, use of computer labs, libraries, or room assignments because of construction or maintenance?
- Are there accreditation or school goals to plan for?
- Who will need a formal evaluation or supervision this year? How many new teachers? How many veterans?
- What is the timeline for doing the first evaluations by what date?
- Have you had a beloved colleague leave and a new person in that spot? How will you support him/her and help the parent community cope?
- Has someone with a lot of institutional history retired? Can any of that knowledge be captured from that person?
- If a teacher is trying out or teaching a singleton class, does the teacher have the necessary materials or need support through an organization or another site?
- Has there been a change in how courses will be taught (for example, ninth-grade science, open enrollment in AP classes, a new team in sixth grade with special education students, a colleague changing from the ELL team to the special education team)? What support does the department chair/grade level/team need to offer those teaching these classes?
- What might the department/grade level/team work on together to improve processes this coming year?
- How might the department/grade level/team work together to develop or refine content in the coming year?
- How could the department/grade level/team work together to teach a specific skill (writing, technology, use of primary sources) in the coming year?
- How might the department/grade level/team work together to teach a student behavior or skill (ethics, stress, character education, social justice, etc.) in the coming year?
- How does the department/grade level/team align with school and district goals (equity, identity safety, social and emotional development of students, differentiation work for gifted and ELL students)?

Additional Topics to Discuss With New Teachers

Although these may not need to be covered in an August orientation, some topics should be covered within the first six weeks or so, sometimes at a generational level. Younger teachers may need support for:

- Communicating with parents.
    - They might need a structure for parent-teacher conferences or ideas for how to handle a difficult e-mail. They may need to know what is best dealt with in writing and what requires a face-to-face discussion.
- Negotiating and conflict management.
    - Young teachers might need to develop skills for better interactions in challenging situations. They often are unprepared for confrontation.
- Norms in staff/department/grade-level meetings.
    - Can one text or knit at a meeting? Is one activity more appropriate than the other? What are the norms for behavior at a meeting at your site? Clarify expectations for *all* the generations. Discussing creating and following norms requires more than this brief space allows, but transparency around norms is essential. Should computers and laptops be closed or not brought to the meeting? Help staff understand why. Be prepared for debate as to what is distracting to different people, different generations.
- Using Facebook or Twitter for communicating with teachers, colleagues, students. Does the district have a policy? Are there or should there be norms? What is and what is not "public" on a school website? On personal social media?
- Protocols. When and with whom do we use first names? Do we interact differently with the superintendent or the board president than our grade-level teacher colleague? E-mails—professional versus personal fonts, using (or not!) emoticons in professional correspondence, avoiding alternative spellings and shorthand, a subject line that tells the person how the e-mail is relevant to them.
- Stress management.
- Etiquette. See Chapter 3.

6 Differentiating Professional Learning for the Generations

Three teachers take a seat in the mandatory professional development induction for new teachers. Ron just graduated and is earning his master's degree in education as he begins his teaching career. Malaya graduated college and then spent several years in the Peace Corps and two years with Teach for America; she has no additional formal teacher preparation classes. Frieda left her career as a social worker after 15 years and received an alternative certification to teach.

These new teachers arrive with vastly different preparation. Their lens on their own learning is affected by those experiences and also by their ages—a young Millennial, an older Millennial, and a Gen Xer. For those preparing teacher professional learning, meeting teachers' needs is as challenging as teachers working to meet student needs—each needs a little something different.

What expectations do different generations have for what and how they learn? What are the differences in their learning styles? What supports do Millennials and Xers need that Boomers don't? How do you make information relevant to them?

THE HOW

When it comes to adult learning, the generations have some things in common. Most teachers, no matter what their generation, want to collaborate—share ideas and talk about their practice (Coggshall et al., 2010). According to Coggshall et al., most also agree that their opportunities to collaborate vary, and half of those surveyed are not satisfied with the opportunities they have.

Professional development should support teachers' desire to collaborate. "All teachers desire meaningful collaboration with their colleagues—not just younger ones," according to the study *Retaining Teacher Talent: The View From*

Generation Y. The report says research in the private sector indicates younger generations strongly value working in teams, forming relationships with coworkers, and forming a relationship with their supervisor. Teachers even put working conditions, including collaboration, ahead of higher pay.

Coggshall et al. write, "Researchers presented a scenario about a hypothetical new magnet school that provided teachers with interactive Smart Boards, high-speed wireless Internet connections, Twitter hotlines and other professional networking opportunities to enhance instruction, technology support staff, and professional development in technology, as well as dedicated time every day for teachers to collaborate with one another. This protected time involved 'sharing lesson plans and instructional strategies, watching DVDs of other teachers teaching the lessons, and networking with teachers at other magnet schools using video- and tele-conferencing. Focus group participants were asked what aspects of this school would be most appealing to them" (2010, p. 28).

Millennials "overwhelmingly" said the most attractive factor of the magnet school to them was the collaboration. In addition to grade-level or department learning teams, collaboration can take the form of opening classroom doors to observe and be observed.

Technology is pushing the boundaries of the site-bound learning community and loosening the restrictions on when, where, and how to access advice. Much more has been written about online communities of practice than can be covered here. Generational differences are most obvious in this area, where digital natives and older tech-lovers cross paths in the Twitterverse, form groups on LinkedIn, and otherwise meet and share advice in cyberspace, sometimes almost instantaneously. A good source of information for professional learning in this area is *The Connected Educator: Learning and Leading in a Digital Age* by Sheryl Nussbaum-Beach and Lani Ritter Hall (Solution Tree, 2011).

> There is such a push-pull difference in the way people relate to information.
>
> In general, the older generation turns on the TV and whatever their chosen news station has for them as the top story, they take in. They "push" a button and what is on is what they get. The younger generation goes online and "pulls" from a bunch of sources. They seek out information. The same can be said for professional development. There are so many blogs and Twitter feeds and Nings and online forums one can choose to participate in and read. Some pull from others across the world. Some wait for professional development day to come a few times a year.–Technology professional developer

Millennials also value and benefit from coaching. Susan Moore Johnson, a professor of education at Harvard University's Graduate School of Education and director of the Project on the Next Generation of Teachers, said new teachers need *coaches* more than *mentors* (2012). Young teachers want meaningful feedback, not just periodic information on how to get more classroom supplies or access information from the human resources department. They want to see their coach in the classroom, not just the lunch line.

Moore Johnson said schools often do a poor job of matching young teachers with mentors and coaches. She said coaches should be selected not just by scheduling convenience but matched by course, grade, subject, or school. The coach's teaching style should be considered, she said, because new teachers may have definite ideas about how they want to teach. Young teachers want to see multiple teaching models, she said.

Good coaching adds value to the school culture and may be a key to recruiting and retaining new young teachers. One caveat: Coaching is a complex art that itself requires multiple skills learned through ongoing professional development.

When matching a coach and coachee, consider the coachee's generation and whether the coach has the necessary understandings to most benefit the person to be coached.

Coaching and Feedback

What might a Boomer want in a coach?

- A coach who has high expectations for both the coach and coachee
- A coach who has deep values around education
- A coach who acknowledges and values prior experience
- A coach who understands that a personal connection matters
- A coach who thinks about the greater goal
- A coach who is mindful of language and how it indicates respect
- A coach who is willing to go the extra mile
- A coach who understands that it is difficult to have to prove oneself again
- A coach who clearly understands the need for clear protocols *and* knows that the coachee can read between the lines

What might an Xer want in a coach?

- A coach who doesn't expect constant face-to-face interaction
- A coach who understands and believes in the life-work balance
- A coach who isn't afraid to answer questions starting with "Why do we have to do . . . ?"
- A coach who doesn't take bluntness personally
- A coach who can be clear and discuss consequences honestly
- A coach who is comfortable with transparency
- A coach who is okay with getting right to business rather than having small talk first
- A coach who understands and doesn't judge when someone just does the work to get it done because of other priorities

What might a Millennial want in a coach?

- A coach who is comfortable with alternative media communication (e-mail, texts, etc.)

(Continued)

(Continued)

- A coach who is open to just-in-time, relevant support and access to materials
- A coach who doesn't patronize
- A coach who recognizes the coachee's knowledge despite the coachee's youth
- A coach who praises the present while seeing a speedy path for the coachee's growth
- A coach who is as willing to take feedback as give it
- A coach who is willing to collaborate and co-create
- A coach who understands if the coachee wants to change jobs or careers

THE WHAT

Professional developers should always recognize the expertise participants bring with them. Professional development leaders need to recognize all the generations in the room and understand their needs. As a leader of a professional learning community, department or grade level, or as a school administrator or district staff developer who facilitates meetings, workshops, or professional development opportunities, consider these generational filters and how they impact your work in designing and leading learning.

Traditionalists

"This is just a fad . . . by the way, my ditto machine is broken. Can you fix it?"

This generation believes that on time is late. Look around a room more than five minutes before a meeting and you'll probably see the majority of those present (if the group has them) are Traditionalists.

They want to get there to sit with their friends. They want to see what information is going to be there, and they want to look over any materials before the meeting starts.

Traditionalists will be better than any other generation with long lectures and less interaction. They know how to sit still and behave well, like the students they were in straight classroom rows with their hands folded on their desks. It isn't that they might not be annoyed by the training but that they are the most patient in practice when it comes to having to sit-and-get.

Their expertise can be a great resource in professional development sessions. Given case studies, Traditionalists can offer insights and help pass along their legacy.

If you're a Traditionalist, understand that later generations want information presented in small bits, want to engage in active or experiential learning, and are less tolerant of lecture-style formats.

Watch your p's and q's with the Traditionalist generation. In one session, an older person pulled Jennifer aside afterward and handed her the session materials—fully edited. The person was sending a message of caring about Jennifer's professionalism.

Grammar and old-fashioned spelling can make a difference even in a more casual context. A recent post on a LinkedIn professional group site said "(I) am lkng to network & shr & glean . . . I'd like yr opinion of yr fave best socialmedia platform. I nd guidance mentoring." The first responder, whose advice was mirrored by several after, wrote, "My best advice involves suggesting that you use standard spelling and punctuation except when you are actually sending a text to someone you know won't be put off."

Boomers

"We did this 20 years ago and I hated it then. Now it's back and you expect me to do what?"

Educators closer to retirement age have a more cyclical perspective. They have seen fads come and go. They are especially impatient with repeating learning they feel they have covered in the past.

Consider alternatives for required information sharing. Can an online video cover how to use an EpiPen? Does training on blood-borne pathogens *need* to be handled face to face?

Team-oriented throughout their youth, this generation wants to work collaboratively, and what the group has to say is important to them. They value social interaction and respect, and they don't like perceived brusqueness. So the Gen Xer who begins a meeting with, "Let's get started" is going to put off Boomers more than someone who opens the session saying, "And how is everyone today?" Even the briefest sincere smile and hello before moving toward the purpose of the exchange makes a big difference. Icebreakers and acknowledgments of key events (birthdays, sports wins, etc.) demonstrate a sense of a community and the group's "we-ness."

This generation likes to use—and hear—the word *we* instead of *I*. Having grown up wanting to make a difference, the idea of *we* is embedded in the Boomer psyche. They believe in the communal best interest and listen for signals of the same value. They believe in education as a calling, so learning that taps into that passion can be especially effective.

If you're a Boomer, understand that Gen Xers value efficiency over group processing and that the generations that follow may not want the close attention you offer for as long as you want to give it.

Learning Characteristics

Traditionalists

- Left-brained, logical
- Appreciate consistency
- May view technology as more trouble than benefit

(Continued)

(Continued)

- Prefer printed summaries
- Generally do not want electronic communication

Boomers

- Interactive learners
- Problem solvers
- See technology as aiding in efficiency but not as a substitute for deep communication and relationship
- Want written materials to scan, but include details
- May be comfortable with some electronic communications with directions

Gen Xers

- Learn by doing
- Enjoy role playing
- Make the technology work to complete the task
- Want bulleted points, graphics, quotes
- Are generally comfortable with online approaches such as websites, blogs, wikis, online surveys
- Want flexibility in work approach
- Want to know that they are learning skills that are transferable (answer What's In It For Me? WIIFM)
- Want to know *why*...

Millennials

- Want to be coached, not mentored
- Appreciate experiential learning
- Want specific, *brief* checklists of what they should do
- Expect that some details will be handled through technology and will go there as a first resort
- Want to work in groups, but desire flexibility in how they approach collaboration
- Want to know the immediate application of what they are learning
- Want time in the meeting to look at the materials; may not prepare ahead
- Need unambiguous expectations
- Can thrive when they are given an area of responsibility

Source: Adapted from Ginsburg (n.d.).

Gen Xers

> *"So help me, if someone says, 'Let's all talk about our vision,' I'm just going to turn around and run."*

Gen Xers, for the most part, want to be told in as efficient and clear language as possible exactly what they are responsible for and then left alone to get it done. Be transparent. Be pragmatic. Then allow them to go about their business. They often are multitaskers, perhaps because they are focused on work-life balance and their lives may involve families and young children.

Gen Xers simply want to know what is on the agenda and why, and what is on their plates and why. This approach makes Gen Xers feel in control, trust the person in charge, and it allows them to move ahead. Balancing Gen Xers' preferences with other generations can be tricky as others can see this expediency as brusqueness or unfriendliness. Conversely, a lot of group discussion will turn off the Gen Xers who see such efforts as schmoozing and a waste of time. Try using protocols to make sure all voices are in the room but explain to the Xers the need.

If you're a Gen Xer, slow down and let others share. Recognize that older generations want consensus and encourage Traditionalists to have their voices be heard. Be careful with Millennials, who may seem confident but often are more fragile and can be put off by what an Xer would view as efficiency. Make sure you are giving Millennials enough detailed specific information and support to do what you expect. Stay present throughout; don't just lay out the expectations and then lay low.

> My credential program is a hybrid model. We only meet once a week in person and then have reading to do online, discussion groups, projects. It is much easier not to have to do all that driving (to get to a meeting), but I don't feel I know the group and that feels strange. I wonder what we are missing in order to have convenience.—Second-grade teacher

Millennials

"What do you want me to do again?"

Millennials appreciate their information nugget-sized. They are technology natives, and social media formats are their norms. In their minds, Twitter's 140 characters are sufficient for most communication. So keep it short. They may not see the value in learning that will meet future needs. For a Millennial, long-term is a year.

Raised in highly supportive environments, Millennials expect to continue to have that kind of support. They want active, hands-on learning, and they prefer to learn in cooperative groups. Team-based experiences will hit their target with this generation, as will information that is visually based. The pragmatic side of the generation will want to see how the learning applies in a real-world setting.

Chapter 1 in Tulgan's *Not Everyone Gets a Trophy: How to Manage Generation Y* (Jossey-Bass, 2009) is titled "Meet Generation Y: The Most High-Maintenance Workforce in the History of the World."

Three of four Millennials in one survey said they would find training more valuable if they could access it through handheld mobile devices. Of those aged 30 to 45, only 40% agreed with that idea, while just 26% of those aged 46 to 65 did. Two-thirds of Millennials thought training sessions should be shorter, compared with 40% of all respondents. And 95% of Millennials said they would value having communications training to become more comfortable talking to managers and supervisors.

Source: Workplace Options, 2011.

Millennials bring fresh energy and vibrancy to the room, but they also bring challenges. They expect a fast pace and for work to be tailored to them rather than the other way around, perhaps because of the scheduled nature of their upbringing. They appreciate coaching, which answers their need for relevant, just-in-time knowledge. Coaching presumes preknowledge, while mentoring is an arm-around-the-shoulders, show-you-the-ropes tactic that can seem patronizing to some Millennials.

Millennials might be under 30, but they also can add *much* to the discussion. Respect what they know and can contribute. Avoid condescending language: "You might not have been here long enough to know this . . . " or "As you are new, you will need to. . . . "

"Just because I am 27 doesn't mean I don't know what I am doing," one Millennial said. We all want to be heard and to feel respected.

If you're a Millennial, be aware that you may have knowledge to share, but so do the other generations. The older generations place a higher premium on experience. Be sure to have all voices heard and set a respectful tone. Be patient.

ACTIVITY 1

Book Study

Plan a book study around the information in the chapters in this text. Identify and use a protocol such as Jigsaw, What/So What?/Now What?, or Save the Last Word to consider just the chapter text.

Many protocols are available from the National School Reform Faculty website at www.nsrfharmony.org.

Alternatively, use the following abbreviated reading list to add to the reading list. Select a reading and use a protocol.

Generation Me: Why Today's Young Americans Are More Confident, Assertive, Entitled—and More Miserable Than Ever Before, by Jean M. Twenge, Free Press, 2006.

Generations at Work: Managing the Clash of Veterans, Boomers, Xers, and Nexters in Your Workplace, by Ron Zemke, Claire Raines, Bob Filipczak, AMACOM, American Management Association, 2000.

"Harnessing the Power of Millennials: New Education Strategies for a Confident, Achieving Youth Generation," by Neil Howe. *The School Administrator,* September 2005.

"Leading Gen Y Teachers: Emerging Strategies for School Leaders," by Ellen Behrstock and Matthew Clifford. *TQ Research & Policy Brief,* February 2009.

"The Lineup of Generations," by Neil Howe. *The School Administrator,* January 2010.

"Long Road to Adulthood Is Growing Even Longer," by Patricia Cohen. *The New York Times,* June 11, 2010.

Managing the Millennials: Discover the Core Competencies for Managing Today's Workforce, by Chip Espinoza, Mick Ukleja, and Craig Rusch, Wiley, 2010.

"The 'Millennials' Are Coming." *60 Minutes,* November 11, 2007 and May 23, 2008. Available at www.cbsnews.com/stories/2007/11/08/60minutes/main3475200.shtml?source=search_story.

Millennials Rising: The Next Great Generation, by William Strauss and Neil Howe, Vintage Books, 2000.

"Talking About Their Generations: Making Sense of a School Environment Made Up of Gen-Xers and Millennials," by William Strauss. *The School Administrator,* September 2005.

When Generations Collide: Who They Are, Why They Clash, How to Solve the Generational Puzzle at Work, by Lynne C. Lancaster and David Stillman, HarperCollins 2002.

ACTIVITY 2

Learning Standards

Learning Forward's Standards for Professional Learning help in understanding the kind of professional learning that can benefit teachers and, through them, their students. Quality professional learning is data-driven, job-embedded, and sustained over time.

Look at the standards with your new generational lens. For each standard, discuss how different generations might view the standard and specifically how each generation might approach meeting that standard. You might divide into generational groups, work in triads, and then report to the group, or you might work through whole-group discussion.

Learning Forward's Standards for Professional Learning

Learning Communities: Professional learning that increases educator effectiveness and results for all students occurs within learning communities committed to continuous improvement, collective responsibility, and goal alignment.

Leadership: Professional learning that increases educator effectiveness and results for all students requires skillful leaders who develop capacity, advocate, and create support systems for professional learning.

Resources: Professional learning that increases educator effectiveness and results for all students requires prioritizing, monitoring, and coordinating resources for educator learning.

Data: Professional learning that increases educator effectiveness and results for all students uses a variety of sources and types of student, educator, and system data to plan, assess, and evaluate professional learning.

Learning Designs: Professional learning that increases educator effectiveness and results for all students integrates theories, research, and models of human learning to achieve its intended outcomes.

Implementation: Professional learning that increases educator effectiveness and results for all students applies research on change and sustains support for implementation of professional learning for long-term change.

Outcomes: Professional learning that increases educator effectiveness and results for all students aligns its outcomes with educator performance and student curriculum standards.

Source: www.learningforward.org

ACTIVITY 3

Scenarios

Robert is the definition of educator. He is energized by working around young people. He arrives early at school each day and often is among the last to leave. He has taken only two sick days in the last 15 years—and one of those was for the death of his father. He's been working in the same school for almost 30 years, and his career as an educator goes back even further. Lately, though, the rate of change has begun to affect him. He just wants to work for a few more years in a job he loves and feels he does well and with great expertise. In fact, the district has named him an outstanding educator twice in his career, and he was a state-level finalist for Teacher of the Year, a fact no one now remembers. This year, he is called each week into a meeting with his colleagues at the high school to discuss what and how they are teaching. Robert attends faithfully but feels disconnected at the meetings. He seldom contributes because he feels no one is listening.

Michelle is a veteran teacher and was recently named department chair. When the district began requiring teachers to work in professional learning teams, she had her concerns. She finds the whole idea, well, *idealistic.* The teachers in this department range in experience from one year to Robert's decades in the classroom. Michelle has accepted the political reality of the situation, however, and is doing her best to lead the meetings. Sometimes she feels less like she is leading and more like she's trying to avert head-on collisions between staff members.

Ashley graduated a year ago from a five-year university teaching program that enabled her to earn her master's degree before beginning her first job here at the school. She's proud of the fact that her university is known as the best education school in the nation. Rather than one year of experience, she views herself as having two years of experience because of that fifth university year. She's brimming with knowledge of the latest research and ideas for changes she just knows would help everyone in the department and school work better with at-risk students, particularly. She often suggests changes when the learning team meets and is increasingly frustrated that the rest of the department is not rallying behind her ideas. In fact, she secretly thinks she'd do a better job as department chair than Michelle is doing.

Reflect

- How might Michelle improve her leadership?
- What might Michelle do to help department members work more cohesively?
- What should Ashley do about her ideas?
- What actions might Robert take to help his department?
- Who else in the department might be available to assist? In what ways?
- How does wearing a generational lens affect the way you view the characters in these scenarios?

7 Succession Planning

It is a common defect in man not to make any provision in the calm against the tempest.

—Machiavelli, *The Prince*, Chapter XXIV

The midsized suburban district's superintendent was meeting with the district's administrators at the end of the school year. The group was smaller than usual. An early retirement incentive had encouraged a number of school administrators and some key central office staff to leave.

The changes led to fitful nights for the superintendent and her cabinet as they frantically worked to fill in the gaps for the next school year. They scrutinized the rosters of assistant principals and asked for recommendations of teacher leaders to seek out, in addition to posting the openings.

At the meeting, the superintendent told the assembled administrators that the next year would be very different.

"You'll have to be patient," she warned. "We've filled a lot of the positions with people who have a lot of energy and are excited about their new roles, but it will take some time for them to get the hang of how we do things. And it will take time for our team to coalesce and get back up to speed."

A new young staff developer turned to her former principal and whispered, "Really! The person I'm supposed to go to for help has been on the job for a year. I don't think I'm going to get the support I would have from the last staff developer." The outgoing staff developer had been in the central office for 25 years.

THE IMPORTANCE OF PLANNING

The teaching population in the United States is older than at any time in the past. Almost half of the K–12 public school teaching force is over age 50, steadily approaching the average teacher retirement age of 59, and by 2020, 1.8 million K–12 teachers and school leaders will be eligible to retire (Foster, 2010).

In 19 years, beginning in 1946 and through 1964, 76 million people were born (Dohm, 2000). Although the Great Recession has spawned dozens of articles about people retiring later, the retirement age was beginning to inch up in the early part of the century after remaining stable for two decades (Dohm, 2000).

The *Monthly Labor Review* (Toossi, 2006) showed the percent of the labor force age 55 and older was expected to creep up through 2020, then begin to decline significantly through 2050. Yet one study found that two-thirds of organizations had no idea of their employees' age profile or when to expect the most retirements (Gravett, n.d.).

As the labor force gets older faster than workers can be replaced—the Boomers are leaving or preparing to, there are not enough Xers to fill the gap, and Millennials are becoming an ever-larger percentage of the educational staff—succession planning is critical. The U.S. Bureau of Labor Statistics predicts that the number of education administrators will increase nearly 15% this decade, while the number of elementary teachers will grow by about 17% and secondary teachers by 6.5% (U.S. Bureau of Labor Statistics, n.d.).

Preparing younger workers for leadership roles is critical. A Boston College Center on Aging and Work survey of 578 companies found that only 33% reported analyzing workplace demographics and having projections about workers' retirement rates (Johnson & Johnson, 2010, p. 218). Another study found an astonishing 66% of companies did not have data on the ages of employees or when impending retirements could affect them (Muson in Gravett & Throckmorton, 2007).

A succession plan identifies the right people to prepare for key positions, seeking those with the qualities and potential to move into leadership positions. Although it is a district's or board's human resource department responsibility to manage talent and support employees' career trajectories, other pressures from outside can be distracting and talent management may be getting short shrift.

Questions of succession are centered on organizing, creating, and capturing the vast knowledge and organizational history that employees take with them as they leave. The culture will change, but the speed with which it changes and whether the change is positive can be dramatically affected by solid succession planning.

Districts and schools need to consider how they are supporting student growth, teacher growth and administrator growth.

- What structures does your district or school have in place to support those who would like to become leaders? A series of teacher leader workshops? A connection to a local administrative program?
- What maps, tools, or professional development abstracts are online for those thinking about leadership?
- What leadership positions have been created so teachers can test their skills at the school site? Team leader? Grade-level leader? Department chair?

(Continued)

(Continued)

Instructional coach? New teacher coach? What skill building is provided for teacher leaders in those positions?

- In what ways are more seasoned teachers (Boomers and Xers) provided structured opportunities to "share the wealth"? To mentor formally or informally?
- What professional learning opportunities do new administrators have? What professional development are experienced administrators offered?
- Do we have a means to identify and maintain the knowledge and experience of retiring staff members?
- Do we have formalized programs that capture key competencies? If we don't, what might such a program look like? What resources do we need for a program like that?
- What are the effects, positive and negative, of staff retiring later? What policies and practices might we have to encourage or discourage later retirements, and what are the benefits of either encouraging or discouraging postponed retirements?

How does a succession plan help?

A Millennial teacher was talking to her Gen-X mentor. She told him, "I see my department chair. I see the principal. I don't want either of those jobs, so I better leave now."

In another conversation, a young teacher was overheard commenting, "I think I might want to be a school leader someday, but no one has told me how to get there."

We cannot say this enough: It is a mistake not to pay attention to the talent management of those newest in our field and those who are Gen Xers as well. School districts need to think creatively to focus on traditional succession planning and the positions that help those moving into leadership roles such as the assistant principalship. Mapping career pathways helps ambitious staff understand what positions will help them to grow and what potential jobs they might have.

- Planning for future leadership helps retain staff.
- Strategizing involves developing people's knowledge, skills, and abilities to be ready to move into key positions. Investing in future leaders can add to their satisfaction and loyalty to the organization.
- Planning ahead helps avoid emergencies. In one state for example, a police scientist with a doctorate was the only one qualified to testify in key court cases involving blood alcohol levels. When she left the position, court cases throughout the state were left in a lurch. Identifying employees with specialized knowledge and skills, such as a special education teacher with counseling training for emotionally impaired elementary students, can avoid panicked searches for the right replacement.
- Succession planning helps ensure cultural norms continue. Protecting high-performing cultures adds to expectations. Making sure traditions and tacit knowledge remain intact helps continue the flow of good performance.

GENERATIONAL DIFFERENCES IN LEADERSHIP STYLES

Part of succession planning is recognizing the strengths of the generations. Leaders from different generations have different styles (Kuhn, 2012). According to Sessa (2007), Boomers and Traditionalists take a more considered approach that draws on others' skills and abilities, while younger leaders are energizing and more focused on short-term results—and more self-focused.

Kuhn finds that Millennials' leadership strengths are that they are rational, selfless, and competent in their leadership style. They view change as positive and desirable, and they think it is important to examine others' ideas and positions. Their training in collaboration is good for building consensus and community, but can be an obstacle to leadership.

Gen Xers are effective leaders in crisis, according to Kuhn (2012). They are perceptive and practical leaders. They are fair and straightforward, and they lead by challenging others' thinking to bring the group into decision making. This generation doesn't want to lead by having meetings and crafting vision statements. They want to eliminate obstacles, leave individuals to do their work on their own, and then offer feedback and share credit. They are perceptive and practical leaders. They are strategic and savvy.

Strauss and Howe (1992) write:

> Gen-X leaders press to simplify the complex, narrow the bloated, and eliminate the unworkable. Their greatest skills are the capacity to observe, to identify unmet needs, to be "smooth" and conceal feelings when necessary, to move quickly when the moment is right, and to make sure that whatever people try does in fact work as intended. They believe that the best way to win is by taking incredible risks. Gen Xers are nobody's fools. If you really need something done, and you don't especially mind how it's done, these are the people to hire. They have the capacity to distinguish between mistakes that matter and those that don't. As leaders, they excel at cunning, flexibility, and deft timing. They are plainspoken, sensible, quick on their feet—and are more inclined to deal than to argue. They are able on-site managers and "behind-the-scenes" facilitators. (p. 416)

Younger Boomers tend to be relational, inclusive, collaborative, task-oriented, and highly productive. They desire global leadership and dedication. They value experience. They have a big-picture orientation. They value listening and encouraging rather than sharing leadership. Kuhn says Boomers are consensus builders who believe in participative leadership. They don't delegate easily. They tend to want to maintain the status quo.

Leadership Differences Among the Generations

Matt Kuhn, a principal consultant with Mid-continent Research for Education and Learning, an education research lab, has studied generational differences and teacher and principal perceptions of change related to the 21 leadership responsibilities from Waters, Marzano, and McNulty (2003).

As part of his study (2012), Kuhn reviewed the literature on generations and generational leadership. Differences in leadership behavior appear in several areas. Boxes left blank did not have enough evidence from the literature. The bolded rows are leadership responsibilities that generations of school leaders tended to be higher or lower in according to the cited publishings.

Leadership Responsibilities	Silent Generation	Baby Boomers	Jones	Generation X	Millennials
Culture: Fosters shared beliefs and a sense of community and cooperation	**High Capacity-** (Strauss & Howe, 1992) **Low Capacity-** (Bishop, 2004; Salahuddin, 2010)	**High Capacity-** (Eslinger, 2000; Eggebeen, 2006) **Low Capacity-** (Strauss & Howe, 1992; Bishop, 2004; Kunreuther, 2008)	**High Capacity-** (Bishop, 2004)	**High Capacity-** (Raines, 1997; Conger, 1998; Woodward, 1999; Goben, 2003; Holman, 2003; Bishop, 2004; Fismer, 2005; Gravett & Throckmorton, 2007; Erickson, 2010) **Low Capacity-** (Strauss & Howe, 1992; Kupperscmidt, 2000; Lancaster & Stillman, 2003)	**High Capacity-** (Strauss & Howe, 1992 & 2000; Alch, 2000; Zemke, Raines, & Filipczak, 2000; Raines, 2003b; Bishop, 2004; Allen, 2004; Martin & Tulgan, 2006; Gravett & Throckmorton, 2007; Editors of New Strategist Publications, 2008)
Order: Establishes a set of standard operation procedures and routines	**High Capacity-** (Strauss & Howe, 1992; Eslinger, 2000; Kupperscmidt, 2000; Raines & Hunt, 2000; Zemke, Raines, & Filipczak, 2000; Lancaster & Stillman, 2003; Bishop, 2004; Lyons, Duxbury, & Higgins, 2005; Martin & Tulgan, 2006; Sessa, 2007)	**High Capacity-** (Eslinger, 2000; Bishop, 2004; Sessa, 2007)	**High Capacity-** (Sessa, 2007)	**Low Capacity-** (Strauss & Howe, 1992 & 2000; Raines, 1997; Martin & Tulgan, 2006; Gordinier, 2008)	**High Capacity-** (Strauss & Howe, 2000; Thielfoldt & Scheef, 2004)

Leadership Responsibilities	Silent Generation	Baby Boomers	Jones	Generation X	Millennials
Discipline: Protects teachers from issues and influences that would detract from their teaching time or focus					**High Capacity-** (Strauss & Howe, 2000)
Resources: Provides teachers with materials and professional development needed to successfully execute their jobs		**High Capacity-** (Deal, Peterson, & Gailor-Loflin, 2001)		**High Capacity-** (Strauss & Howe, 1992; Powell, 2003)	**High Capacity-** (Spears, 1995; Gage, 2005) **Low Capacity-** (Powell, 2003)
Involvement in curriculum, instruction, and assessment: Is directly involved in designing and implementing curriculum, instruction, and assessment practices			**High Capacity-** (Bishop, 2004)	**High Capacity-** (Deal, Peterson, & Gailor-Loflin, 2001; Sessa, 2007; Salahuddin, 2010)	**High Capacity-** (Gage, 2005)
Focus: Establishes clear goals and keeps those goals in the forefront of the school's attention	**High Capacity-** (Kupperscmidt, 2000; Zemke, Raines, & Filipczak, 2000; Lancaster & Stillman, 2003; Bishop, 2004)	**High Capacity-** (Kiechel, 1989; Bishop, 2004; Lyons, Duxbury, & Higgins, 2005)	**High Capacity-** (Wong, 2000; Sessa, 2007)	**High Capacity-** (Hladun, 1990; Arsenault, 2004; Martin & Tulgan, 2006; Gravett & Throckmorton, 2007; Sessa, 2007)	**High Capacity-** (Strauss & Howe, 1992; Zemke, Raines, & Filipczak, 2000; Martin & Tulgan, 2001; Raines, 2003b; Arsenault, 2004; Sessa, 2007)

(Continued)

(Continued)

Leadership Responsibilities	Silent Generation	Baby Boomers	Jones	Generation X	Millennials
Knowledge of curriculum, instruction, and assessment: Is knowledgeable about current curriculum, instruction, and assessment practices	**High Capacity-** (Strauss & Howe, 1992; Sessa, 2007)	**High Capacity-** (Sessa, 2007)	**High Capacity-** (Sessa, 2007)	**High Capacity-** (Hladun, 1990; Losyk, 1997a, 1997b; Raines, 1998; Cufaude, 2000; Kupperscmidt, 2000; Zemke, Raines, & Filipczak, 2000; Deal, Peterson, & Gailor-Loflin, 2001; Hessen & Lewis, 2001; Holman, 2003; Muetzel, 2003; Sessa, 2007; Editors of New Strategist Publications, 2008)	**High Capacity-** (Strauss & Howe, 1992; Sessa, 2007)
Visibility: Has quality contact and interactions with teachers and students			**Low Capacity-** (Fink & Brayman, 2006)	**Low Capacity-** (Fink & Brayman, 2006)	
Contingent rewards: Recognizes and rewards individual accomplishments		**High Capacity-** (Holman, 2003)		**High Capacity-** (Raines, 1997; Cole, 1999; Woodward, 1999; Muetzel, 2003; Chan, 2005; Fismer, 2005; Lyons, Duxbury, & Higgins, 2005)	**High Capacity-** (Lancaster & Stillman, 2003; Chan, 2005; Lyons, Duxbury, & Higgins, 2005; Martin & Tulgan, 2006; Gravett & Throckmorton, 2007; Coggins, 2010)
Communication: Establishes strong lines of communication with teachers and among students	**High Capacity-** (Strauss & Howe, 1992; Conger, 1998)	**High Capacity-** (Holman, 2003)	**High Capacity-** (Sessa, 2007)	**High Capacity-** (Strauss & Howe, 1992: Muchnik, 1996; Holman, 2003; Muetzel, 2003; Fismer, 2005)	
Outreach: Is an advocate and spokesperson for the school to all stakeholders					**Low Capacity-** (Lovely, 2010)

Leadership Responsibilities	Silent Generation	Baby Boomers	Jones	Generation X	Millennials
Input: Involves teachers in designing and implementing important decisions and policies	**High Capacity-** (Strauss & Howe, 1992; Martin & Tulgan, 2006; Sessa, 2007) **Low Capacity-** (Conger, 1998; Kupperscmidt, 2000; Zemke, Raines, & Filipczak, 2000; Lancaster & Stillman, 2003; Gravett & Throckmorton, 2007; Salahuddin, 2010)	**High Capacity-** (Wagenknecht-Ivey, 1997; Deal, Peterson, & Gailor-Loflin, 2001; Powell, 2003; Gravett & Throckmorton, 2007; Sessa, 2007)	**High Capacity-** (Bishop, 2004; Sessa, 2007)	**High Capacity-** (Raines, 1997; Cole, 1999; Hays, 1999; Woodward, 1999; Tulgan, 2000; Goben, 2003; Muetzel, 2003; Miller & Yu, 2005; Gravett & Throckmorton, 2007; Sessa, 2007; Salahuddin, 2010)	**High Capacity-** (Raines, 2003b; Martin & Tulgan, 2006; Gravett & Throckmorton, 2007; Ruggeri, 2009)
Affirmation: Recognizes and celebrates school accomplishments and acknowledges failures		**High Capacity-** (Sessa, 2007)		**High Capacity-** (Woodward, 1999; Zemke, Raines, & Filipczak, 2000) **Low Capacity-** (Gordinier, 2008)	**High Capacity-** (Strauss & Howe, 1992; Martin & Tulgan, 2001; Lancaster & Stillman, 2002; Markley, 2002)
Relationship: Demonstrates an awareness of the personal aspects of teachers and staff	**High Capacity-** (Strauss & Howe, 1992; Arsenault, 2004; Martin & Tulgan, 2006)	**High Capacity-** (Eslinger, 2000; Raines & Hunt, 2000; Arsenault, 2004)	**High Capacity-** (Muller, 1997; Bishop, 2004)	**High Capacity-** (Wong, 2000; Miller & Yu, 2005)	**High Capacity-** (Strauss & Howe, 1992; Raines, 2003b; Gage, 2005; Gravett & Throckmorton, 2007; Sessa, 2007)
Change agent: Is willing to and actively changes the status quo	**Low Capacity-** (Clarke, 1970; Strauss & Howe, 1992; Zemke, Raines, & Filipczak, 2000)	**High Capacity-** (Hludan, 1990; Holman, 2003) **Low Capacity-** (Lovely, 2010)	**High Capacity-** (Martin & Tulgan, 2006)	**High Capacity-** (Strauss & Howe, 1992; Rosen, 2001; Goben, 2003; Holman, 2003; Muetzel, 2003; Bishop, 2004; Martin & Tulgan, 2006; Kunreuther, 2008; Salahuddin, 2010)	**High Capacity-** (Lovern, 2001; Sandfort & Haworth, 2001; Powell, 2003; Lyons, Duxbury, & Higgins, 2005; Martin & Tulgan, 2006; Kunreuther, 2008) **Low Capacity-** (Strauss & Howe, 2000)

(Continued)

(Continued)

Leadership Responsibilities	Silent Generation	Baby Boomers	Jones	Generation X	Millennials
Optimize: Inspires and leads new and challenging innovations		**High Capacity-** (Eslinger, 2000; Holman, 2003; Arsenault, 2004)	**High Capacity-** (Coll, 2007) **Low Capacity-** (Strauss & Howe, 1992)	**High Capacity-** (Strauss & Howe, 1992 & 2000; Raines & Hunt, 2000; Deal, 2001; Holman, 2003; Powell, 2003; Arsenault, 2004; Bishop, 2004; Martin & Tulgan, 2006; Sessa, 2007; Erickson, 2010)	**High Capacity-** (Powell, 2003; Lyons, Duxbury, & Higgins, 2005; Sessa, 2007)
Ideals/beliefs: Communicates and operates from strong ideals and beliefs about schooling	**High Capacity-** (Eslinger, 2000; Kupperscmidt, 2000; Zemke, Raines, & Filipczak, 2000; Lancaster & Stillman, 2003; Lyons, Duxbury, & Higgins, 2005)	**High Capacity-** (Strauss & Howe, 1992 & 2000; Lyons, Duxbury, & Higgins, 2005)		**High Capacity-** (Gravett & Throckmorton, 2007)	**High Capacity-** (Gage, 2005)
Monitors and evaluates: Monitors the effectiveness of school practices and their impact on student learning	**High Capacity-** (Kupperscmidt, 2000; Zemke, Raines, & Filipczak, 2000; Lancaster & Stillman, 2003) **Low Capacity-** (Strauss & Howe, 1992)	**Low Capacity-** (Hladun, 1990)		**High Capacity-** (Hladun, 1990; Conger, 1998; Raines, 1998; Woodward, 1999; Tulgan, 2000; Raines & Hunt; 2000; Goben, 2003; Gravett & Throckmorton, 2007)	**High Capacity-** (Gravett & Throckmorton, 2007; Coggins, Zuckerman, & McKelvey, 2010)
Flexibility: Adapts his or her leadership behavior to the needs of the current situation and is comfortable with dissent	**High Capacity-** (Strauss & Howe, 1992) **Low Capacity-** (Gravett & Throckmorton, 2007)	**Low Capacity-** (Martin & Tulgan, 2006; Gravett & Throckmorton, 2007)	**High Capacity-** (Martin & Tulgan, 2006)	**High Capacity-** (Strauss & Howe, 1992; Raines, 1997; Conger, 1998; Hays, 1999; Woodward, 1999; Tulgan, 2000; Buckley et al., 2001; Deal, Peterson, & Gailor-Loflin 2001; Goben, 2003; Muetzel, 2003; Thielfoldt & Scheef, 2004)	**High Capacity-** (Gage, 2005; Martin & Tulgan, 2006) **Low Capacity-** (Strauss & Howe, 2000; Twenge & Campbell, 2008)

Leadership Responsibilities	Silent Generation	Baby Boomers	Jones	Generation X	Millennials
Situational awareness: Is aware of the details and undercurrents in the running of the school and uses this information to address current and potential problems	**High Capacity-** (Strauss & Howe, 1992)			**High Capacity-** (Strauss & Howe, 1992; Raines, 1998; Tulgan, 2000; Martin & Tulgan, 2006; Kunreuther, 2008; Erickson, 2010)	
Intellectual stimulation: Ensures faculty and staff are aware of the most current theories and practices and makes the discussion of these a regular aspect of the school's culture	**High Capacity-** (Strauss & Howe, 1992)	**High Capacity-** (Holman, 2003; Sessa, 2007)		**High Capacity-** (Holtz, 1995; Clurman, 1997; Raines, 1997; Conger, 1998; Elsdon, & Iyer 1999; Munk, 1999; Goben, 2003; Holman, 2003; Chan, 2005; Lyons, Duxbury, & Higgins, 2005; Editors of New Strategist Publications, 2008)	**High Capacity-** (Powell, 2003; Lyons, Duxbury, & Higgins, 2005; Martin & Tulgan, 2006)

A MODEL OF SUCCESSION PLANNING

Good succession planning involves the active support of top leaders, links planning to the district strategic plan, identifies talent early in the employee's career, offers more than formal training by giving employees challenges that stretch their learning, addresses diversity, champions change, and incorporates employee input, according to a study from the Institute for Education Leadership (The Learning Partnership, 2008, p. 11). The institute offers resources for succession planning and talent development (*http://appliki.apandrose.com/*).

"The best succession planning practices are proactive," according to a model in Ontario, Canada. "Talented individuals are identified early and nurtured throughout their careers through professional development that is integrated into human resource management" (The Learning Partnership, 2008, p. 11).

The province developed a framework for growth with input from education partners and leadership experts that is evidence-based. Ontario schools focus on five areas, termed Core Leadership Capacities. These have been recognized by research, practitioners, and education partners as critical areas of leadership required for sustained improvement in student achievement and well-being. In each area, in addition to outlining the concept, a rubric describes how implementation, capacity building, and sustaining capacity look. The continuum helps districts identify their implementation and set goals.

- **Identification and recruitment.** Districts are called on to develop leadership profiles, create a plan to help potential leaders self-assess their skills using specific tools, collect and analyze data on the system's needs, develop specific strategies to address diversity, and actively provide potential leaders with opportunities to experience the role.
- **Training and developing aspiring leaders.** Districts need to outline what skills and knowledge a position requires and offer aspiring leaders opportunities to "observe the use of and acquire the competencies outlined in the leadership profile" (Ontario Ministry of Education, 2011, p. 44). Training and development provide professional growth in the competencies.
- **The selection process.** The district must outline different pathways to leadership roles that encourage leaders with a variety of backgrounds. The process should be "accommodating to a variety of learning styles" (Ontario Ministry of Education, 2011, p. 45) so that it is inclusive, and the district has identified potential biases and barriers within the process and worked to overcome them.
- **Professional learning for leaders.** Districts must offer training and resources to new leaders, provide mentoring and informal support from retirees or those who were promoted, and evaluate their processes for supporting instructional leaders. Experienced leaders' learning opportunities are set through learning networks, self-assessments, and other learning opportunities. Performance appraisals based on the leadership profiles are integral to leaders' professional learning.
- **Placement and transfer processes.** Policies and procedures align with association guidelines. Districts also must develop and communicate transition processes for both incoming and outgoing leaders and have short-term coaching in place for incoming leaders on enhancing performance, reflecting on practice, or examining and solving an issue.

The province understands the ultimate reason for succession planning and makes it clear in a manual that every board must follow: "The progress and success of all students in Ontario is contingent on having effective leadership at every level to guide and support teaching and learning in Ontario schools. We need effective directors, academic superintendents, business superintendents, principals, vice-principals, and managers in order to support teacher excellence, create outstanding schools, and foster student achievement and well being. A board leadership development strategy enables boards to attract and develop leaders of the highest quality" (Ontario Ministry of Education, 2011, p. 3).

ACTIVITY 1

District Assessment for Developing Aspiring Leaders

Objective: To review existing supports for aspiring leaders and consider areas that could be strengthened.

Time: 30 minutes.

Materials: A copy of the chart for each group member.

In the box on the right side of the chart, identify how aspiring leaders in your district or school would know about and find support to take advantage of the opportunities listed.

Experience writing curriculum.	
Leadership in teachers' association.	
Attendance at regional, state, or national learning conference.	
Connection with community partners, such as businesses or youth service organizations.	
Participation in book studies.	
Participation in action research.	
Training in communication skills.	
Gaining skills to work with constituencies, particularly families.	
Learning about national and global education trends.	
Cross-grade and/or cross-school study of curriculum.	
Examination of student work.	
Data analysis.	
Knowledge and understanding of the needs of adult learners and models of professional learning.	
Facilitating groups, including knowledge of effective teamwork.	
Ability to give and receive feedback.	
Skills in conflict management and effective use of conflict.	
Peer coaching.	
Shadowing leaders.	
Mentoring new teachers or preservice candidates.	
Understanding of socioeconomic and cultural differences, including discriminatory practices.	

Developing technology skills to support student and adult learning experiences.	
Opportunities to lead professional learning.	
Facilitate a group.	
Learn to access, analyze, and interpret data.	
Participate in peer observation.	
Learn to use evidence to evaluate student performance.	
Understand school etiquette and proper procedures.	
Understand the school board's role.	
Know different roles and responsibilities, and explain the career paths to those roles; demonstrate understanding of the system.	
Manage the budget of a school or department program.	
Manage school resources and operations, such as through participation on school leadership team.	
Participate on a principal or teacher selection committee.	
Familiar with state and district learning frameworks, such as curricula area standards.	
Knowledgeable about school procedures, such as for emergency response, misconduct, etc.	
Develop oral and written skills.	

Use the blank boxes to add additional responsibilities and explain how the school or district supports aspiring leaders in developing those.

As a group, discuss the following:

- Which areas are strengths?
- Which could be improved?
- How well does the district or school support aspiring leaders overall?

Sources: Adapted from the Institute for Education Leadership (2013) and the Ontario Ministry of Education (2011).

ACTIVITY 2

Aspiring Leader Self-Assessment

Objective: To determine your own strengths and identify areas to focus on to become a leader.

Time: 15 minutes.

Materials: A copy of the list.

If you plan a career that includes administrative opportunities or a leadership role, assess how well you are preparing for increased responsibilities. The suggestions below are an incomplete list of opportunities to develop leadership skills. They are nonsuccessive and do not need to be addressed in order.

Place a check next to each statement that matches your experience.

Curriculum Design/Lesson Study/Analysis of Student Work/Professional Learning

___ I have participated in writing curriculum.

___ I have worked with peers at different grade levels to examine curricular needs.

___ I have participated in peer observation, through lesson study or walk-throughs.

___ I have participated in a professional book study with my teaching colleagues.

___ I have taken part in action research.

___ I have evaluated my own students' performance based on thorough review of various data.

___ I have analyzed student work alongside colleagues.

___ I have worked with peers in different schools to examine student needs or other districtwide concerns.

___ I have participated in a professional book study with my teaching colleagues.

___ I have attended a regional, state, or national professional learning conference.

___ I have a deep understanding of socioeconomic and cultural factors that influence student learning.

___ I use social networking for my own professional learning.

___ I have evaluated my own students' performance based on thorough review of various data.

___ I have participated on a districtwide or statewide committee to design curricula, standards, or otherwise frame an educational issue.

Adult Learning and Meeting Facilitation

___ I have taken part in some form of professional learning about meeting the needs of adult learners and different models of professional development.

___ I have facilitated a group.

___ I have designed a meeting or professional learning opportunity.

___ I have been a department chairperson.

___ I have provided peer feedback.

___ I have studied conflict management and how to use conflict effectively.

___ I have taken part in communications training.

___ I have mentored new teachers or preservice candidates.

___ I have led professional learning for colleagues in my school or district, or an external group of educators.

___ I have participated in peer observation, through lesson study or walk-throughs.

___ I have been a peer coach.

___ I have developed skills in questioning, paraphrasing, and so on to be able to coach others.

___ I am an effective writer.

___ I am a good speaker.

School/District Leadership

___ I have served in a leadership position with my teachers' association.

___ I have worked on a school-related issue with a community partner.

___ I have worked with peers to analyze data.

___ I have read and understand the district antidiscrimination policies and procedures.

___ I have led an accreditation committee.

___ I communicate with parents in a variety of ways.

___ I understand the proper etiquette for in-school communications, including the lines of authority for regular tasks, how and when to approach support staff and supervisors.

___ I have served on a principal or teacher selection committee.

___ I am familiar with my school's emergency response protocol.

___ I have been part of a school-wide council or a member of the school leadership team.

Understanding the Perspective of School and District Leaders

___ I can identify different groups that the position to which I aspire interacts with, and I am able to state concerns and interests each group is likely to have in school matters.

___ I have reviewed the role and responsibilities of the position to which I aspire, for example, by getting the official job description.

___ I have discussed career paths with a knowledgeable authority.

___ I have shadowed a leader.

___ I have studied professional literature on national and global education trends.

___ I have attended a school board meeting to observe and/or speak.

Consider the following:

- What other leadership skills not on the above list do you think are necessary for the position you desire? List them, and check those that describe you.
- How many checks do you have?
- In what areas might you improve your leadership skills?
- What actions will you take next to develop your leadership?

Sources: Adapted from the Institute for Education Leadership (2013) and the Ontario Ministry of Education (2011).

ACTIVITY 3

Capture the Institutional History

Objective: To maintain and enhance staff understanding of the school or district history and culture and to respect retirees' institutional knowledge.

- Ask a retiring teacher to contribute one page to a scrapbook that describes a school tradition that was the most meaningful to that person.
- Ask a committee of volunteers to interview retiring teachers and generate some historical record. The interview might be recorded in a written record or on a videotape.

Some questions might be:

- How were teachers oriented when you were a new teacher?
- What school traditions have you most valued?
- What was the most significant contribution to your professional learning?
- What do you wish would change?
- What do you wish wouldn't change?
- What advice would you give to new teachers?

- Ask retiring teachers to leave a letter for an incoming teacher. Leave the subject open for the teacher to decide whether the contents are advice or history.

Source: T. Farrell, personal communication, April 2011.

ACTIVITY 4

Case Study

Read the case study. Consider similarities and differences with your district as you read. Underline the similarities and circle the differences. Discuss what you mark with colleagues.

Consider these questions:

1. What structures does your district or school have in place to support those who would like to become leaders? A series of teacher leader workshops? A connection to a local administrative program?
2. What maps, tools, or professional development abstracts are online for those thinking about leadership to review?
3. What leadership positions have been created so teachers can test their skills at the school site? Team lead? Grade-level lead? Department chair? English language learner coach? Instructional coach? New teacher coach? What skill building is provided for teacher leaders in those positions?
4. In what ways are more seasoned teachers (Boomers and Xers) provided structured opportunities to "share the wealth"? To mentor formally or informally?

CASE STUDY: HALEY

Haley is in her third year working for a suburban school. She has finished her new-teacher program, in which she met colleagues across the district, learned about district initiatives, improved her planning, instruction and assessment, self-reflected constantly, and worked one-on-one with a coach several times a month.

This year she has done some good work with her professional learning community on meeting the needs of her English learners, advised a lunchtime club, and gotten to know her school beyond just her classroom even better.

Haley finds herself really liking both her students and her colleagues. Both the adults and the kids interest her. She volunteers for sharing a best practice at a staff meeting and agrees to sit on the professional development committee at the school. She has even been invited to attend a state conference. Her colleagues say she is a go-getter (in a good way), and she begins to think of herself as a teacher leader. She smiles when she considers that title, proud of her contributions. As the school year finishes, Haley thinks she'd like to learn more about this "leadership stuff." Where to go?

Haley has found herself in an excellent school board that supports both student and teacher learning, and she learns that the board has a bunch of online resources to help her figure out what she might want to do next.

She logs into her intradistrict site and scouts out the section on Leadership Development on the human resources page. The site has a grid that shows all the learning opportunities there are for aspiring leaders, those who are just in their first formal leadership positions, and other opportunities for experienced leaders both on the certificated as well as the classified side of the district. Haley is delighted that her district has thought through what supports they want to provide at every step of someone's career.

Haley clicks on the link for aspiring leaders, and there she finds a list of job descriptions for instructional coaches, tech integration specialists, and curriculum consultants, as well as those for vice principal and principal. She scans the job descriptions to see what piques her interest. What might she want to become next?

In the Professional Development section of the aspiring leader page, she also notices a link. In looking through it, she spots PDFs she can download. One is a self-assessment tool she can look at to see what skills her district believes a good leader has. Haley can assess what she already does quite well and what skills she might need to develop within herself. The good news is that right in the same area of the website is a list of leadership workshops that fit her specific needs. The first one is this summer, a "What Are My Steps to Becoming an Educational Leader?" workshop including a series of sessions with folks from the district office who help aspiring leaders learn about themselves, their emotional intelligence quotient, and their leadership capabilities. Terrific.

Haley reads on. Instead of being overwhelmed, Haley is thrilled. There is a continuum of support. She keeps reading the words "talent management." She likes to be thought of as having talent. She reads that after she identifies herself as an aspiring leader, the next step is to have a meeting with her administrator around a self-assessment. She and her principal can review what is needed to become a leader, and Haley can develop her own growth plan. She can attend workshops that will develop her skill sets and take inventories to learn about her capabilities and where she needs to grow.

On the website, Haley also sees that there are possibilities for a mentor once in a leadership position—a "new leader" coach. Then there are also possibilities for shadowing at the district office to see what administrators do in their roles, an opportunity to join book talks, conduct action research, and even participate in an exchange to another school. And there is a university close by that has a cohort of principal candidates finishing administrative credentials in her district.

Haley knows a few of her colleagues who have participated in some of the training and she also knows her new assistant principal came up through the ranks of her school. "They do encourage us to grow," Haley smiles to herself happily. "I can see myself here for a while."

Epilogue

Normally in the course of professional learning, the culminating activity is some amalgam or interpretation of a "Here's What, So What, Now What" exercise. In the final session, everyone has a chance to summarize key ideas learned and why those insights are important in a professional context. Then each participant lists a few "Now What?" next steps. What will I do or say differently than I might have before the professional development began? What changes will I make to my practice?

This book is the "Here's What." This is what we know about the generations and how generational similarities and differences make the workplace more interesting—and more challenging.

You likely picked up this book with some ideas in the back of your mind that are the "So What" of generational savvy. You probably were aware of some differences in your workplace or elsewhere that led you to question what was happening. We hope through the examples we shared, the facts and information we provided, and the discussions you generated by working through the activities you selected in each chapter, that your "So What?" awareness has grown. What you read and what you might have learned in discussions with your colleagues we hope helped you develop your generational filter of perception to see how generational differences affect your work.

Now we come to "Now What?" What specifically will you change in your practice?

- How will you communicate in a way that better supports how you interact with a different generation?
- Will you change your website in ways that meet the needs of the generation you are recruiting?
- Will you start planning professional learning with a more nuanced generational lens?
- Are you prepared to look at your legacy to thoughtfully plan how best to prepare those who will take your position?

As we said in the introduction and throughout the book, the generational filter is *only one* filter through which to see ourselves and our work. Working effectively together also requires taking into account colleagues' cultures, racial, and ethnic affiliations; countries of origin; genders; religious identifications; and other filters through which we view the world. This book asks that you add the generational lens.

So what will you do next with your increased awareness and understanding of the generations? What will you do differently as a teacher and a colleague? As a principal? As a system or district administrator? What will move you and your work forward to act with greater understanding and effectiveness? The answer lies in the generational savvy you acquired in the process of working through this material, additional readings you may have sought out, and the generational dexterity that you now apply.

Bibliography and References

60 Minutes. (2007, November 11, and 2008, May 23). *The 'Millennials' are coming.* Retrieved from http://www.cbsnews.com/stories/2007/11/08/60minutes/main 3475200.shtml?source=search_story.

Alch, M. (2000). Get ready for the Net Generation. *Training and Development, 54*(2), 32–34.

Allen, P. (2004). Welcoming Y. *Benefits Canada, 28*(9), 51–53.

Alsop, R. (2008). *The trophy kids grow up: How the Millennial generation is shaking up the workplace.* San Francisco, CA: Jossey-Bass.

American Association of Retired People. (1995). *Valuing older workers: A study of costs and productivity.* Washington, DC: Author.

Armour, S. (2005, November 6). Generation Y: They've arrived at work with a new attitude. *USA Today.*

Arsenault, P. M. (2004). Validating generational differences: A legitimate diversity and leadership issue. *The Leadership & Organization Development Journal, 25,* 124–141.

Bane, V. (2008, July 7). The littlest cubicle warriors: Forget daycare, now parents can bring their babies to work. *People.*

Belkin, L. (2008, June 15). When Mom and Dad share it all. *The New York Times.*

Bennis, W. G., & Thomas, R. J. (2002). *Geeks and geezers: How era, values, and defining moments shape leaders.* Cambridge, MA: Harvard Business School Press.

Bishop, C. (2004). *Generational cohorts and cultural diversity as factors affecting leadership transition in organizations.* Deerfield, IL: Trinity Evangelical Divinity School.

Block, M. (2009, October 29). VFW post makes push to recruit young vets. NPR: *All Things Considered.*

Brandon, R., & Seldman, M. (2004). *Survival of the savvy: High-integrity politics for career and company success.* New York, NY: Free Press.

Braunschweiger, J. (2010, September). *Attack of the woman-dominated workplace.* Retrieved from http://www.more.com/reinvention-money/careers/attack-woman-dominated-workplace.

Brooks, D. (2009, November 3). Cellphones, texts and lovers. *The New York Times.*

Bryner, J. (2010, March 10). Big generation gaps in work attitudes revealed. *Live Science.* Retrieved from http://www.livescience.com/6195-big-generation-gaps-work-attitudes-revealed.html.

Buchanan, L. (2010, September). Meet the Millennials. *INC, 32*(7), 166.

Buckleitner, W. (2008, June 12). So young, and so gadgeted. *The New York Times.*

Buckley, M. R., Beu, D. S., Novicevic, M. M., & Sigerstad, T. D. (2001). Managing generation next: Individual and organizational perspectives. *Review of Business, 22*(1/2), 81–85.

CareerBuilder. (2010). *More than four-in-ten workers over the age of 35 currently work for a younger boss, finds new CareerBuilder survey.* Retrieved from http://www.careerbuilder.com/share/aboutus/pressreleasesdetail.aspx?id=pr554&sd=2/17/2010&ed=12/31/2010&siteid=cbpr&sc_cmp1=cb_pr554_.

Carr, N. (2008, July/August). Is Google making us stupid? *The Atlantic, 301*(6).

Carroll, T. G. (2007). *Policy brief: The high cost of teacher turnover.* Washington, DC: National Commission on Teaching and America's Future.

Catalyst. (2012). *Catalyst quick take: Generations in the workplace in the United States & Canada.* New York, NY: Catalyst.

Chan, D. S. H. (2005). *Relationship between generation-responsive leadership behaviors and job satisfaction leadership behaviors and job satisfaction of generations X and Y professionals.* Ann Arbor, MI: University of Phoenix–ProQuest Information and Learning.

Clarke, G. (1970, June 29). The Silent generation revisited. *Time Magazine.*

Clurman, J. W. (1997). *Rocking the ages.* New York, NY: Harper Business.

Coggins, C., Zuckerman, S., & McKelvey, L. A. (2010). Holding on to gen Y. *Educational Leadership,* 70–74.

Coggshall, J. G., Behrstock-Sherratt, E., & Drill, K. (2011, April). *Workplaces that support high-performing teaching and learning: Insights from Generation Y teachers.* Naperville, IL, and Washington, DC: American Institutes for Research and the American Federation of Teachers.

Coggshall, J. G., Ott, A., Behrstock, E., & Lasagna, M. (2010). Retaining teacher talent: The view from Generation Y. Naperville, IL, and New York, NY: Learning Point Associates and Public Agenda.

Cohen, P. (2008, July 3). The '60s begin to fade as liberal professors retire. *The New York Times.*

Cohen, P. (2010, June 11). Long road to adulthood is growing even longer. *The New York Times.*

Cole, J. (1999, November). The art of wooing gen-Xers. *HR Focus,* 7–8.

Coll, J. (2007). *Generation Jones.* Retrieved from http://www.generationjones.co.uk/gen_jones.

Conger, J. A. (1998, January 1). *How Gen-X managers manage. Strategy + Business,* 10.

Cufaude, J. B. (2000). Eager to attract more young people into your association membership? Here's the rhetoric and the reality about generational differences. *Association Management, 52*(1), 73–80.

Deal, J. J. (2007). *Retiring the generation gap: How employees young and old can find common ground.* San Francisco, CA: Jossey-Bass.

Deal, J. J., Peterson, K., & Gailor-Loflin, H. (2001). *Emerging leaders.* Greensboro, NC: Center for Creative Leadership.

Dee, J. (2008, September 21). The tell-all campus tour. *The New York Times.*

Dohm, A. (2000, July). Gauging the labor force effects of retiring baby-boomers. *Monthly Labor Review,* 17–25.

Douglas, E. (2012, November 6). *Succession planning 101.* Retrieved from http://blogs.edweek.org/topschooljobs/k-12_talent_manager/2012/11/succession_planning_101.html.

Eckert, R. (2013, April). The two most important words. *The Harvard Business Review.*

Editors of New Strategist Publications. (2008). *American generations.* Ithaca, NY: New Strategist Publications.

Eggebeen, D. J. (2006). Demography of the Baby Boomers. In S. L. Susan Krauss Whitbourne (Ed.), *The Baby Boomers grow up* (pp. 3–22). Mahwah, NJ: Lawrence Erlbaum Associates.

Elliott, S. (2009). *Ties to tattoos: Turning generational differences into a competitive advantage.* Dallas, TX: Brown Books.

Elsdon, R., & Iyer, S. (1999). Creating value and enhancing retention through employee development: The Sun Microsystems experience. *Human Resource Planning, 22,* 39–47.

Erickson, T. J. (2010). The leaders we need now. *Harvard Business Review.*

Eslinger, M. R. (2000). *A multi-generational workplace: The differentiation of generations by the work values they possess.* Moscow: University of Idaho.

Espinoza, C., Ukleja, M., & Rusch, C. (2010). *Managing the Millennials: Discover the core competencies for managing today's workforce.* Hoboken, NJ: Wiley.

Families and Work Institute. (2004). *Generation & gender in the workplace.* Watertown, MA: American Business Collaboration.

Fernandez-Araoz, C., Groysberg, B. & Nohria, N. (2009, May). The definitive guide to recruiting in good times and bad. *Harvard Business Review.*

Fink, D., & Brayman, C. (2006). School leadership succession and the challenges of change. *Educational Administration Quarterly, 42*(1), 62–89.

Fismer, E. C. (2005). *Generation X leadership styles and job satisfaction in the information technology consulting industry.* Dallas, TX: University of Phoenix.

Foster, E. (2010). *How Boomers can contribute to student success: Emerging encore career opportunities in K–12 education.* Washington, DC: National Commission on Teaching and America's Future.

Freedman, M. (2007). *Encore: Finding work that matters in the second half of life.* New York, NY: Public Affairs.

Friedman, T. L. (2007, October 10). Generation Q. *The New York Times.*

Gage, A. J. (2005). *A phenomenological study of the leadership perceptions of the G.I. and Millennial generations.* Lincoln: University of Nebraska.

GfK Custom Research. (2011). *Young workers disengaged by pressures of work worldwide.* Retrieved from http://www.gfkamerica.com/newsroom/press_releases/single_sites/008030/index.en.print.html.

Gibbs, N. (2009, November 20). The growing backlash against overparenting. *TIME Magazine* in partnership with CNN.

Ginsburg, D. (n.d.). *Teaching across the generations: Challenges and opportunities for preceptors.* Austin: The University of Texas at Austin.

Goben, A. (2003). *The X factor: Generation X Leadership in early 21st century American community colleges.* Austin: The University of Texas at Austin.

Gordinier, J. (2008). *X saves the world.* London, England: Penguin Books Limited.

Gordon, D. T. (2002, July/August). Fuel for reform: The importance of trust in changing schools. *Harvard Education Letter, 18*(4).

Gostick, A. & Elton, C. (2009). *The carrot principle: How the best managers use recognition to engage their people, retain talent, and accelerate performance.* New York, NY: Free Press.

Gravett, L. (n.d.). *Retention is not a one size fits all proposition.* Retrieved from http://www.gravett.com/articles/2008/08–9.htm.

Gravett, L., & Throckmorton, R. (2007). *Bridging the generation gap: How to get Radio Babies, Boomers, Gen Xers, and Gen Yers to work together and achieve more.* Franklin Lakes, NJ: Career Press.

Hafner, K. (2007, June 17). The boys in the band are in AARP. *The New York Times.*

Hayes, D. (2008). *Anytime play date: Inside the preschool entertainment boom, or how television became my baby's best friend.* New York, NY: Free Press.

Hays, S. (1999, November). Generation X and the art of the reward. *Workforce*, 44–48.

Helft, M. (2007, March 10). Google's buses help its workers beat the rush. *The New York Times.*

Helft, M. (2007, May 28). In fierce competition, Google finds novel ways to feed hiring machine. *The New York Times.*

Hessen, C. N., & Lewis, B. J. (2001, Winter). Steps you can take to hire, keep, and inspire generation Xers. *Leadership and Management in Engineering*, 42–44.

Hladun, H. (1990). The Class of '90: Today's graduates need special handling. *Canadian Business, 63*(3), 99–100.

Hoffman, J. (2008, June 22). Does 8th-grade pomp fit the circumstance? *The New York Times.*

Holman, R. (2003). *Identifying and comparing differences in the values of elementary school principals among Baby Boomers and generation Xers.* La Verne, CA: University of La Verne.

Holson, L. M. (2008, March 9). Text generation gap: U R 2 Old (JK). *The New York Times.*

Holtz, G. T. (1995). *Welcome to the jungle: The why behind generation X.* New York, NY: St. Martin's Press.

Howe, N. (2005, September). Harnessing the power of Millennials: New education strategies for a confident, achieving youth generation. *The School Administrator.*

Howe, N. (2008. December 7). The kids are alright. But their parents. . . . *The Washington Post.*

Howe, N. (2010a, January). The lineup of generations. *The School Administrator, 1*(67), 20–21.

Howe, N. (2010b, January). Meet Mr. and Mrs. Gen X: A new parent generation. *The School Administrator, 1*(67), 18–23.

Howe, N., & Strauss, W. (2007, July/August). The next 20 years: How customer and workforce will evolve. *Harvard Business Review.*

Huntley, R. (2006). *The world according to Y.* Crows Nest, NSW, Australia: Allen & Unwin.

Ingersoll, R. M. (2012, May). Beginning teacher induction: What the data tell us. *Phi Delta Kappan, 93*(8), 47–51.

Ingersoll, R. M., & Merrill, L. (n.d.). *The changing face of the teaching force.* Retrieved from http://www.gse.upenn.edu/review/feature/ingersoll.

The Institute for Education Leadership. (2013). *Self-assessment tool for aspiring leaders.* Ontario, Canada: Author.

Jacobs, A. (2008, June 22). Blame the messenger: When sending an e-vite, expect evasion. *The New York Times.*

James, J. B., Swanberg, J. E., & McKechnie, S. P. (2007). *Generational differences in perceptions of older workers' capabilities* (Issue in Brief #12). Chestnut Hill, MA: The Center for Aging and Work/Workplace Flexibility at Boston College.

Jayson, S. (2010, November 18). Other generations growing weary of Baby Boomers. *USA Today.*

Johnson, L. (2006). *Mind your X's and Y's: Satisfying the 10 cravings of a new generation of customers.* New York, NY: Free Press.

Johnson, M., & Johnson, L. (2010). *Generations, Inc.: From Boomers to Linksters—Managing the friction between generations at work.* New York, NY: AMACOM.

Jones, D. (2008, July 22). Can the fist bump mix with business? *USA Today.*

Kantrowitz, B., & Tyre, P. (2006, May 22). The fine art of letting go. *Newsweek.*

Keen, A. (2007). *The cult of the amateur: How today's Internet is killing our culture.* New York, NY: Doubleday/Currency.

Keigher, A., & Cross, F. (2010, August). *Teacher attrition and mobility: Results from the 2008–09 teacher follow-up survey.* Washington, DC: National Center for Education Statistics.

Kelley, T. (2008, July 27). Dear parents: Please relax, it's just camp. *The New York Times.*

Kiechel, W. (1989, April 10). The workaholic generation. *Fortune,* 50–62.

Kopkowski, C. (2008, April). Why they leave: Lack of respect, NCLB, and underfunding—In a topsy-turvy profession, what can make today's teachers stay? *NEA Today.*

Kuhn, M. (2012). *Leading schools through a generational lens: Perceptions of principals' change leadership disaggregated by principal generation* (ProQuest Dissertations & Theses Document ID 1023814803). Retrieved from http://search.proquest.com//docview/1023814803.

Kunreuther, F. (2008). *Working across generations: Defining the future of nonprofit leadership.* San Francisco, CA: Jossey-Bass.

Kupperscmidt, B. (2000). Multigenerational employees: Strategies for effective management. *Health Care Manager, 19,* 65–76.

Kuz, M. (2007, May 2). Boomtastrophe: Baby Boomers hoped to die before they got old. They lied. And now they're dragging the whole country down. *SF Weekly.*

Labash, M. (2008, March–April). Are we having fun yet? The infantilization of corporate America. *The Weekly Standard.*

Lancaster, L. C., & Stillman, D. (2002). *When generations collide: Who they are, why they clash, how to solve the generational puzzle at work.* New York, NY: HarperCollins.

Lancaster, L. C., & Stillman, D. (2003). *When generations collide.* New York, NY: Collins Business.

Lancaster, L. C., & Stillman, D. (2010). *The M-factor: How the Millennial generation is rocking the workplace.* New York, NY: HarperCollins.

Larsen, B. (2006). *Understanding generational differences: Build relationships better by understanding generational diversity.* A presentation for Winona State University, Winona, MN.

The Learning Partnership. (2008). *Succession planning for Ontario schools and school boards: A study commissioned by the Institute for Education Leadership.* Ontario, Canada: Institute for Education Leadership. Retrieved from http://www.education-leadership-ontario.ca/storage/2/1284604393/SuccessionPlanningSummary.pdf.

Leland, J. (2010, April 24). A graying population, a graying work force. *The New York Times.*

Lenhart, A. (2009). *Social networks grow.* Washington, DC: Pew Research Center. Retrieved from http://www.pewinternet.org/~/media//Files/Reports/2009/PIP_Adult_social_networking_data_memo_FINAL.pdf.pdf.

Levine, A., & Dean, D. R. (2012). *Generation on a tightrope: A portrait of today's college student.* San Francisco, CA: Jossey-Bass.

Lewis, G. B., & Cho, Y. J. (2011). The aging of the state government workforce: Trends and implications. *American Review of Public Administration, 41*(1), 48–60.

Lipkin, N. A., & Perrymore, A. J. (2009). *Y in the workplace: Managing the "me first" generation.* Franklin Lakes, NJ: The Career Press.

Losyk, B. (1997a). Generation X: What are they like? *Current,* 9–13.

Losyk, B. (1997b). Generation X: What they think and what they plan to do. *The Futurist,* 39–44.

Lovely, S. (2005, September). Creating synergy in the schoolhouse: Changing dynamics among peer cohorts will drive the work of school systems. *The School Administrator.*

Lovely, S. (2010, January 1). Generations at school: Building an age-friendly workplace. *The School Administrator,* 10–16.

Lyons, S., Duxbury, L., & Higgins, C. (2005). An empirical assessment of generational differences in work-related values. *Proceedings of the Annual Conference of the Administrative Sciences.* Toronto, Canada.

Marantz Henig, R. (2010, August 18). What is it about 20-somethings? *New York Times Magazine.*

Markley, D. (2002). Here comes Y. *Successful Meeting.*

Martin, C. A., & Tulgan, B. (2006). Managing the generation mix: From urgency to opportunity. Amherst, MA: HRD Press.

Marvel, J., Lyter, D. M., Peltola, P., Strizek, G. A., Morton, B. A., & Rowland, R. (2007, January). *Teacher attrition and mobility: Results from the 2004–05 teacher follow-up survey.* Washington, DC: National Center for Education Statistics.

Marx, P. (2012, October 8). Golden years: How will boomers handle retirement? Hire an expert. *The New Yorker.*

Maslin Nir, S. (2010, November 19). No boo-boos or cowlicks? Only in school pictures. *The New York Times.*

McBride, T. & Nief, R. (2013). The Mindset List. Beloit College. Retrieved from http://www.beloit.edu/mindset/

McGinn, D. (2006, June 19). Second time around, in The Boomer Files. *Newsweek.*

Merkin, D. (2007, May 6). The way we live now: Reinventing middle age. *The New York Times.*

MetLife. (2009). *The MetLife Survey of the American Teacher: Collaborating for student success.* New York, NY: Author.

Miller, P., & Yu, H. C. (2005). Leadership style—The X Generation and Baby Boomers compared in different cultural contexts. *Leadership & Organization Development Journal, 26*(1), 35–50.

Moore Johnson, S. (2012, December). Remarks made at the Learning Forward Annual Conference, Boston, MA.

Moore Johnson, S., Harrison Berg, J., Donaldson, M. L. (2005, February). *Who stays in teaching and why: A review of the literature on teacher retention.* Cambridge, MA: The Project on the Next Generation of Teachers, Harvard Graduate School of Education.

Muchnick, M. (1996). *Naked management: Bare essentials for motivating the X Generation at work.* Boca Raton, FL: St. Lucie Press.

Muetzel, M. (2003). *They're not aloof . . . Just Generation X.* Shreveport, LA: Steel Bay Publishing.

Muller, T. E. (1997). The benevolent society: Value and life style changes among middle-aged Baby Boomers. In L. R. Kahle (Ed.), *Values, lifestyles, and psychographics* (pp. 299–316). Mahwah, NJ: Lawrence Erlbaum Associates.

Munk, N. (1999). Finished at forty. *Fortune,* 50–66.

NAS Recruitment Communications. (2006). *Generation Y: The Millennials: Ready or not, here they come* (NAS Insights). Cleveland, OH: Author. Retrieved from http://www.scribd.com/doc/2607132/GENERATION-Y-THE-MILLENNIALS.

National Center for Education Statistics. (2002). *Schools and Staffing Survey, 1999–2000: Overview of the data for public, private, public charter, and bureau of Indian affairs elementary and secondary schools.* Washington, DC: U.S. Department of Education.

Ontario Ministry of Education. (2011). *Board leadership development strategy requirements manual.* Ontario, Canada: Author. Retrieved from http://www.edu.gov.on.ca/eng/policyfunding/leadership/BLDS2012Manual.pdf.

Parker, A. (2010, May 2). *All the Obama 20-somethings.* Retrieved from http://www.nytreprints.com.

PBS Frontline. *Growing up online.* Retrieved from http://www.pbs.org/wgbh/pages/frontline/kidsonline/.

Pentland, A. (2012, April). The new science of building great teams. *Harvard Business Review.* Retrieved from http://hbr.org/2012/04/the-new-science-of-building-great-teams/ar/1.

Pew Research Center. (2009). *Recession turns a graying office grayer.* Washington, DC: Pew Research Center. Retrieved from http://pewsocialtrends.org/assets/pdf/americas-changing-workforce.pdf.

Pew Research Center. (2010a). *The Millennials: Confident. Connected. Open to change.* Washington, DC: The Pew Research Center. Retrieved from http://pewresearch.org/millennials/.

Pew Research Center. (2010b). *Millennials: A portrait of Generation Next.* Retrieved from http://pewsocialtrends.org/assets/pdf/millennials-confident-connected-open-to-change.pdf.

Pitt-Catsouphes, M., Smyer, M. A., Matz-Costa, C., & Kane, K. (2007). The national study report: Phase II of the national study of business strategy and workforce development (Research Highlight No. 04). Chestnut Hill, MA: The Center on Aging & Work/Workplace Flexibility. Retrieved from http://agingandwork.bc.edu/documents/RH04_NationalStudy_03–07_004.pdf.

Population Reference Bureau. (2008, June). U.S. labor force trends. *Population Bulletin, 63*(2), 1–17.

Powell, J. N. (2003). *Generational perceptions of effective leadership.* Sarasota, FL: Argosy University.

Prensky, M. (2008, June/July). Young minds, fast times: How tech-obsessed ikids would improve our schools. *Edutopia.*

Public Agenda. (2000). *A sense of calling: Who teaches and why.* Retrieved from http://www.publicagenda.org/specials/teachers/teachers.htm.

Public Agenda. (2010). *Retaining teacher talent.* New York, NY: Author.

Quindlen, A. (2006, May 29). A cubicle is not a home. *Newsweek.*

Raines, C. (1997). *Beyond Generation X: A practical guide for managers.* Menlo Park, CA: Crisp Publications.

Raines, C. (2003a). *Connecting generations: The sourcebook for a new workplace.* Menlo Park, CA: Crisp Publications.

Raines, C. (2003b). Generations at work: Managing Millennials. In C. Raines (Ed.), *Connecting generations: The sourcebook for a new workplace.* Menlo Park, CA: Crisp Publications.

Raines, C., & Hunt, J. (2000). *The Xers and the Boomers from adversaries to allies: A diplomat's guide.* Menlo Park, CA: Crisp Publications.

Ranstad Work Solutions. (2007). *The world of work 2007.* Rochester, NY: Harris Interactive. Retrieved from http://us.randstad.com/content/aboutrandstad/knowledge-center/employer-resources/World-of-Work-2007.pdf.

Randstad Work Solutions. (2008). *The world of work 2008.* Rochester, NY: Harris Interactive. Retrieved from http://us.randstad.com/content/aboutrandstad/knowledge-center/employer-resources/World-of-Work-2008.pdf.

Randstad Work Solutions. (2012). *Personal contact preferred.* Retrieved from http://www.randstad.com/press-room/research-reports.

Ravinale, L. (n.d.). Working effectively with others [Worksheet]. Santa Cruz, CA: Ordinary Magic Life and Business Coaching.

Rich, M. (2008, July 27). Literacy debate: Online, R U really reading? *The New York Times.*

Richtel, M. (2010, November 21). Growing up digital, Wired for distraction. *The New York Times.*

Rosenbloom, S. (2007, April 5). Mommy and Daddy's little life coach. *The New York Times.*

Rosenbloom, S. (2008, January 17). Generation Me vs. You revisited. *The New York Times.*

Ruggeri, A. (2009, November 1). The Youth movement; Confident, entrepreneurial, and socially conscious, generation Y begins to show the sure—if just a bit different—makings of leadership. *U.S. News and World Report*, p. 30.

Ryan, R. (n.d.). *The next generation's Rotary Club.* Retrieved from http://www.worthwhilemag.com/Articles/nexgenrotary.aspx.

Sacks, D. (2006, January). Scenes from the culture clash. *Fast Company.*

Salahuddin, M. M. (2010). Generational differences impact on leadership style and organizational success. *Journal of Diversity Management, 5*(2).

Scelfo, J. (2008, February 14). Parent shock: Children are not décor. *The New York Times.*

Schworm, P. (2008, January 7). Colleges turn to web tools in hunt for '08 freshmen. *The Boston Globe.*

Seligson, H. (2008, August 31). Girl power at school, but not at the office. *The New York Times.*

Sessa, V. K. (2007). Generational differences in leader values and leadership behaviors. *The Psychologist-Manager Journal, 10*(1).

Shaffer, J. (2008). *Gen Y talent: How to attract and retain the young and the restless* (white paper). Redwood Shores, CA: Saba. Retrieved from http://www.saba.com/resources/whitepapers/saba_wp_gen_y_talent.pdf.

Shapira, I. (2008, July 6). What comes after Generation X? As a demographic, Millennials don't all see it as the best label. *Washington Post.*

Shapiro, W. (2009, October 6). *You talkin' to me? A primer on Boomer speak.* Retrieved from http://www.politicsdaily.com/2009/10/06/you-talkin-to-me-a-primer-on-boomer-speak/.

Shellenbarger, S. (2007, April 30). Read this and weep: Crying at work gains acceptance. *Wall Street Journal.*

Smith, W. S. (2008). *Decoding generational differences: Fact, fiction . . . or should we just get back to work?* New York, NY: Deloitte Development.

Society for Human Resource Management. (2003, December). *2003 generational differences survey report.* Alexandria, VA: E. M. Burke.

Spears, L. (1995). Servant leadership and the Greenleaf legacy. In *Reflections on leadership* (pp. 1–14). New York, NY: Wiley.

Stone, B. (2010, April 22). For web's new wave, sharing details is the point. *The New York Times.*

Strauss, W. (2005, September). Talking about their generations: Making sense of a school environment made up of Gen-Xers and Millennials. *The School Administrator.*

Strauss, W., & Howe, N. (1992). *Generations: The history of America's future, 1584 to 2069.* New York, NY: Quill William Morrow.

Strauss, W., & Howe, N. (2000). *Millennials rising: The next great generation.* New York, NY: Vintage Books.

Sujansky, J. G., & Ferri-Reed, J. (2009). *Keeping the Millennials: Why companies are losing billions in turnover to this generation and what to do about it.* Hoboken, NJ: Wiley.

Sweeney, C. (2008, February 28). Never too young for that first pedicure. *The New York Times.*

Sweeney, C. (2008, September 11). Twittering from the cradle. *The New York Times.*

Taylor, P., Morin, R., Parker, K., & Wang, W. (2009). Growing old in America: Expectations vs. reality. Washington, DC: Pew Research Center. Retrieved from http://www.pewsocialtrends.org/files/2010/10/Getting-Old-in-America.pdf.

Thielfoldt D., & Scheef, D. (2004, August 1). Generation X and The Millennials: What you need to know about mentoring the new generations. *Law Practice Today.*

Tolbize, A. (2008). *Generational differences in the workplace.* Minneapolis: University of Minnesota, Research and Training Center.

Toossi, M. (2002, May). A century of change: The U.S. labor force, 1950–2050. *Monthly Labor Review,* 15–28.

Toossi, M. (2006, November). A new look at long-term labor force projections to 2050. *Monthly Labor Review,* 19–39.

Trunk, P. (2007, July 11). *Why we should be grateful for Gen Y.* Retrieved from http://blog.penelopetrunk.com/2007/07/12/yahoo-column-why-we-should-be-grateful-for-generation-y/.

Tulgan, B. (2000). *Managing Generation X: How to bring out the best in young talent.* New York, NY: Norton.

Tulgan, B. (2009). *Not everyone gets a trophy: How to manage Generation Y.* San Francisco, CA: Jossey-Bass.

Tutelian, L. (2008, August 22). Following the kids to college. *The New York Times.*

Twenge, J. M. (2006). *Generation Me: Why today's young Americans are more confident, assertive, entitled— and more miserable than ever before.* New York, NY: Free Press.

Twenge, J. M., & Campbell, K. (2008). Increases in positive self-views among high school students: Birth-cohort changes in anticipated performance, self-satisfaction, self-liking, and self-competence. *Psychological Science, 19*(11), 1082–1086.

Tyler, K. (2013, January). Job worth doing: Update descriptions. *HR Magazine, 58*(1).

U.S. Bureau of Labor Statistics. (n.d.). Employment by industry, occupation, and percent distribution, 2010 and projected 2020 [Excel data file]. Washington, DC: Author.

Van Gelder, L. (2011, February). *Mom, Dad, I'm home.* Retrieved from http://www.more.com/reinvention-money/money/mom-dad-im-home.

Wagenknecht-Ivey, B. (1997). *Values of Boomers and Busters in the workplace.* Denver, CO: University of Denver Department of Social Sciences.

Waters, J. T., Marzano, R. J., & McNulty, B. (2003). *Balanced leadership: What 30 years of research tells us about the effect of leadership on student achievement.* Aurora, CO: Mid-continent Research for Education and Learning.

Watters, E. (2003). *Urban tribes: A generation redefines friendship, family and commitment.* New York, NY: Bloomsbury.

Weeks, L. (2007, July 6). The eye generation prefers not to read all about it: Students in film class—A microcosm of a visually oriented culture. *The Washington Post.*

Welch, S. (2008, March). Can you work this weekend? *O, The Oprah Magazine.*

Williams, A. (2008, February 10). Look who's getting rolled out of the bar. *The New York Times.*

Williams, A. (2008, April 27). Not-so-personal finance. *The New York Times.*

Winerip, M. (April 29, 2007). Young, gifted, and not getting into Harvard. *The New York Times.*

Winograd, M., & Hais, M. D. (2008). *Millennial makeover: MySpace, YouTube & the future of American politics.* Piscataway Township, NJ: Rutgers University Press.

Wong, L. (2000). *Generations apart: Xers and Boomers in the officer corps.* Carlisle, PA: Strategic Studies Institute, U.S. Army War College.

Woodward, N. H. (1999, March). The coming of the managers. *HR Magazine, 44*(3), 74–80.

Workplace Options. (2011). *Millennials face uphill battle to wow co-workers with work ethic.* Retrieved from http://www.workplaceoptions.com/news/press-releases/press-release.asp?id=E42B752BC8BB4DE293E8&title=%20Millennials%20Face%20Uphill%20Battle%20to%20Wow%20Co-Workers%20with%20Work%20Ethic.

Zaslow, J. (2007, April 20). The most-praised generation goes to work. *US Edition Business Online.*

Zemke, R., Raines, C., & Filipczak, B. (2000). *Generations at work: Managing the clash of Veterans, Boomers, Xers, and Nexters in your workplace.* New York, NY: AMACOM.

Zimmerman, E. (2008, August 3). When that screen starts to look smaller. *The New York Times.*

Zoby, J. (2008). *The way we'll be: The Zogby Report on the transformation of the American dream.* New York, NY: Random House.

Zukin, C., & Szeltner, M. (2012). *Net Impacts' talent report: What workers want in 2012.* Brunswick, NJ: Heldrich Center, Rutgers University. Retrieved from http://www.heldrich.rutgers.edu/sites/default/files/content/Net_Impact_Talent_Report.pdf.

Index